Anonymous

Minutes of the General Council of Medical Education and Registration

of the United Kingdom. Vol. 9

Anonymous

Minutes of the General Council of Medical Education and Registration *of the United Kingdom. Vol. 9*

ISBN/EAN: 9783337298418

Printed in Europe, USA, Canada, Australia, Japan

Cover: Foto ©Suzi / pixelio.de

More available books at **www.hansebooks.com**

MINUTES

OF THE

GENERAL COUNCIL

OF

MEDICAL EDUCATION & REGISTRATION

OF THE

UNITED KINGDOM;

OF THE

EXECUTIVE COMMITTEE:

AND OF THE

BRANCH COUNCILS,

FOR THE YEAR 1871.

VOL. IX.

London:

PRINTED BY W. J. & S. GOLBOURN, PRINCES STREET,
COVENTRY STREET. W.

1872.

GENERAL COUNCIL

OF

MEDICAL EDUCATION & REGISTRATION.

MEETING OF TUESDAY, JULY 4TH, 1871.

President—Dr. GEORGE EDWARD PAGET.

The Royal College of Physicians of London . . .	Dr. JAMES RISDON BENNETT.
The Royal College of Surgeons of England	RICHARD QUAIN, Esq.
The Apothecaries' Society of London	GEORGE COOPER, Esq.
The University of Oxford . .	Dr. HENRY WENTWORTH ACLAND.
The University of Cambridge .	Dr. GEORGE MURRAY HUMPHRY.
The University of Durham . .	Dr. DENNIS EMBLETON.
The University of London . .	Dr. JOHN STORRAR
The Royal College of Physicians of Edinburgh . .	Dr. ALEXANDER WOOD.
The Royal College of Surgeons of Edinburgh	Dr. ANDREW WOOD.
The Faculty of Physicians and Surgeons, Glasgow . . .	Dr. JOHN GIBSON FLEMING.
The Universities of Aberdeen and Edinburgh	Dr. JOHN MACROBIN.
The Universities of Glasgow and St. Andrew's . . .	Dr. ALLEN THOMSON.

The King and Queen's College
of Physicians in Ireland . Dr. AQUILLA SMITH.
The Royal College of Surgeons
in Ireland . . . . . . WILLIAM HARGRAVE, Esq.
The Apothecaries' Hall of Ireland . . . . Dr. CHARLES HENRY LEET.
The University of Dublin . . Dr. JAMES APJOHN.
The Queen's University in Ireland . . . . Sir DOMINIC CORRIGAN, Bart.

Dr. EDMUND ALEXANDER PARKES.
Dr. RICHARD QUAIN.
Dr. WILLIAM SHARPEY.
Dr. WILLIAM WITHEY GULL.
Dr. ROBERT CHRISTISON.
Dr. WILLIAM STOKES.
} Nominated by Her Majesty, with the advice of her Privy Council.

Dr. FRANCIS HAWKINS, *Registrar*.

(No. 140.)

GENERAL COUNCIL
OF
MEDICAL EDUCATION & REGISTRATION.

MINUTES OF MEETING, TUESDAY, JULY 4, 1871.

32, SOHO SQUARE, LONDON, W.

Present—

Dr. PAGET, *President*, in the Chair.

Dr. BENNETT.	Mr. HARGRAVE.
Dr. ACLAND.	Dr. LEET.
Dr. HUMPHRY.	Dr. APJOHN.
Dr. EMBLETON.	Sir D. CORRIGAN, Bart.
Dr. STORRAR.	Dr. QUAIN.
Dr. ALEXANDER WOOD.	Dr. SHARPEY.
Dr. ANDREW WOOD.	Dr. GULL.
Dr. FLEMING.	Dr. PARKES.
Dr. MACROBIN.	Dr. CHRISTISON.
Dr. THOMSON.	Dr. STOKES.
Dr. A. SMITH.	

Dr. FRANCIS HAWKINS, *Registrar.*

The Minutes of the last Meeting were read and confirmed.

1. *Read*—The following official notification :

"14th *July*, 1870.

"We, the Royal College of Surgeons of England, in pursuance of the power given to us by the Medical Act, do hereby appoint Mr. RICHARD QUAIN to be a Member of the General Council of Medical Education and Registration of the United Kingdom, for the term of five years from the 14th day of July, 1870.

"In witness whereof the said Royal College of Surgeons of England have caused their Common Seal to be affixed the 14th day of July, 1870."

Mr. QUAIN was then introduced by Dr. BENNETT.

2. *Read*—The following official notification :

"AT THE COURT AT WINDSOR, THE 29TH DAY OF JUNE, 1871.

Present—
The Queen's Most Excellent Majesty in Council.

"Her Majesty in Council was this day pleased, by and with the advice of Her Privy Council, in pursuance of the provisions contained in the 4th Section of the 21st and 22nd Victoria, c. 90, to appoint WILLIAM WITHEY GULL, Esquire, M.D., to be for five years a Member of the General Council of Medical Education and Registration in the United Kingdom, in the place of HENRY WYLDBORE RUMSEY, Esquire, M.D., resigned.

(Signed) "ARTHUR HELPS."

Dr. GULL was then introduced by Dr. STOKES.

3. The following Committees were appointed :

Business Committee.

Dr. ANDREW WOOD, *Chairman.*
Dr. EMBLETON.
Dr. A. SMITH.
Dr. LEET.

Finance Committee.

Dr. SHARPEY, *Chairman.*
Dr. BENNETT.
Dr. QUAIN.
Dr. A. SMITH.
Dr. FLEMING.

Committee on the Registration of Medical Students, and the Returns from the Bodies in Schedule (A), *of Professional Examinations and their Results.*

Dr. EMBLETON, *Chairman.*
Dr. FLEMING.
Dr. A. SMITH.

4. The following Returns from the Medical Department of the Army, and from the Military Department of the India Office, were laid before the Council:

ARMY MEDICAL DEPARTMENT.
30th March, 1871.

SIR,

With reference to previous correspondence, I have the honour to transmit a Statement of the Degrees, Diplomas, and Licences of the Candidates for Commissions in the Medical Department of the Army, who in February last presented themselves for Examination.

I have the honour to be,
SIR,
Your obedient Servant,
(Signed) T. G. LOGAN,
Director-General.

THE REGISTRAR,
Medical Registration Office,
32, Soho Square, W.

INDIA OFFICE, S.W.,
1st February, 1871.

SIR,
I am directed by the Secretary of State for India in Council to forward a Statement of the Degrees, Diplomas, and Licences of the Candidates for Commissions in the Medical Department of the Indian Army, who, in February 1870, presented themselves for Examination at Chelsea Hospital.

No Examination has taken place since that date.

I am, SIR,
Your obedient Servant,
(Signed) T. T. PEARS,
Major-General, Military Secretary.

THE REGISTRAR,
*General Council of Medical Education
and Registration.*

STATEMENT *of the Degrees, Diplomas, and Licences of the Candidates for Commissions in the Medical Department of the Army, who, in February 1871, presented themselves for Examination, showing the number that passed, and did not pass, distinguishing the Qualifications, both Medical and Surgical, under the heads of the several Licensing Bodies.*

NAMES OF LICENSING BODIES.		Total	Number passed	Number failed	Deficient in Anatomy	Deficient in Surgery	Deficient in Medicine	REMARKS.
Royal Coll. of Physicians, London	Licentiates	3	3	...	...	...	...	
Ditto Surgeons, England	Members	12	12	...	...	...	...	
The Society of Apothecaries, London	Licentiates	8	8	...	...	...	...	
Royal Coll. of Physicians, Edinburgh	Do.	10	9	1	1	1	...	CANDIDATES.
Ditto Surgeons, Edinburgh	Do.	10	9	1	1	1	...	
K. and Q. Coll. of Physicians, Ireland	Do.	14	11	3	2	3	1	Successful 36
Royal Coll. of Surgeons, Ireland	Do.	18	15	3	2	3	1	Unsuccessful . . . 21
Apothecaries' Hall, Dublin	Do.	3	3	...	...	...	...	——
University of Edinburgh	M.B.	2	2	...	...	...	...	Total . . . 57
Ditto Glasgow	M.B.	2	2	...	...	...	...	——
Ditto ditto	M.Ch.	2	2	...	...	...	...	
Ditto Aberdeen	M.B.	4	4	...	...	...	...	
Ditto ditto	M.Ch.	4	4	...	...	...	...	
Queen's University, Ireland	M.D.	8	8	...	...	...	...	Of the unsuccessful, seventeen would have been accepted had there been vacancies for them.
Ditto ditto	M.Ch.	6	6	...	...	...	...	
University of Dublin	M.B.	5	5	...	...	...	...	
Ditto ditto	M.Ch.	3	3	...	...	...	...	
Ditto ditto	Lic. in Med.	1	1	...	...	...	...	
Ditto ditto	Lic. in Surg.	1	1	...	...	...	...	
TOTAL		116	108	8	6	8	2	

STATEMENT of the Degrees, Diplomas, and Licences of the Candidates for Commissions in the Medical Department of the Indian Army, who, in February 1870, presented themselves for Examination, showing the number that passed, and did not pass, distinguishing the Qualifications, both Medical and Surgical, under the heads of the several Licensing Bodies.

NAMES OF LICENSING BODIES.	QUALIFICATIONS.			Deficient in		REMARKS.
	No. of Qualifications.			Medicine.	Anatomy, Operative Surgery, and Surgery.	
	Total	No. passed.	No. failed.			
Royal College of Surgeons, England . . Members	2	1	1			CANDIDATES.
Ditto ditto Ireland . . . Licentiates	9	3	6			Successful 10
College of Physicians, Ireland . . . . Ditto	2	1	1			Failed 13
King and Queen's College of Physicians,⎫ Ditto	6	1	5	1		
Ireland . . . .⎭						Total . . 23
Queen's University, Ireland . {Licentiates	1	1				
{Doctor in Medicine	2	2			*	DIPLOMAS & DEGREES.
University of Dublin . . . {Bachelor of Medicine	1		1			
{Master in Surgery	1	1				Successful 21
{Members	1		1			Failed 26
Ditto Aberdeen . . . {Master in Surgery	2	1	1			
Ditto Glasgow . . . {Bachelor in Medicine	2	1	1		†	Total . . 47
{Master in Surgery	1		1			
Ditto Edinburgh . {Bachelor of Medicine	4	3				* 2 Deficient in all subjects.
{Master in Surgery	4	3	1			† 1 Ditto Ditto.
Royal College of Physicians, Edinburgh . Licentiates	5	1	4			N.B.—Of the 13 Candidates returned as unsuccessful, 9 were qualified, but were not accepted, as only 10 appointments were made.
Ditto Surgeons ditto . . Ditto	4	1	3			
TOTAL	47	21	26	1		

Moved by Sir DOMINIC CORRIGAN; *Seconded* by Dr. ANDREW WOOD; and *Agreed to:*

> "That the Returns from the Medical Departments of the Army, and of the Indian Army, be entered on the Minutes."

5. The List of Examining Bodies, whose Examinations fulfil the conditions of the Medical Council as regards Preliminary Education, which had been prepared by the Executive Committee, was laid before the Council.

It was the same as the List of last year, with the following addition, viz.:

> "*The Examiners for Commissions in the Military and Naval Services of the United Kingdom:*
>
> "*Certificate to include all the subjects required by the General Medical Council.*"

Moved by Mr. HARGRAVE; *Seconded* by Dr. PARKES; and *Agreed to:*

> "That the List of Examining Bodies, with the proposed addition, be approved."

6. *Moved* by Dr. PARKES; *Seconded* by Dr. STORRAR; and *Agreed to:*

> "That the Report of the Committee of the Council on Professional Education be received and entered on the Minutes."

REPORT.

THE Report of the Committee of 1869 on Professional Education, and the replies to the letter of the Chairman from Teachers on Medical Education, were forwarded to the Licensing Bodies, and answers were received from them in 1870.

All the answers did not arrive in time to be presented at the Meetings of Council in 1870, and accordingly an *interim* report only was then laid before the Council (Minutes, Vol. viii. p. 11). By a Resolution of Council (Minutes, Vol. viii. p. 105), the Committee on Education was reappointed, and directed to report at a future Meeting of the Council.

Subsequently replies to the first Education Report having been received from all the Licensing Bodies, they were printed and distributed, last autumn, to the Members of Council, and are contained in the Appendix to the 8th Volume of the Minutes of the Meetings of the Council.

The probability that an Act to regulate Medical Education would be passed in 1870, rendered it inexpedient to discuss last year many of the suggestions contained in the Education Report, and in the replies sent in by the Licensing Bodies, for if the Medical Bill of 1870 had been passed, it would have necessitated a revision of the whole subject of Medical Education and Examination, and would have rendered any previous decisions null and void.

During the last two years very important alterations have been made in the system of Education and Examination by some of the Licensing Bodies, and several of the suggestions of the Education Committee have been met.

The Royal College of Physicians of London, by a rule passed in April, 1871, requires from every Candidate for its Licence, evidence that he has discharged the duties of Clinical Clerk, and of Dresser, for periods of three months respectively, and thus one important recommendation of the Education Report has been carried out.

The Royal College of Surgeons of England, on the reception of the Report, appointed a Committee to consider it, and eventually determined to act on the opinion of their Court of Examiners of the 16th December, 1869, that "every part of the knowledge included in, or accessory to, the Education of Candidates for the Diplomas of the College ought to be taught and learnt practically." The College has, therefore, introduced into its Curriculum clauses which insure practical instruction in Chemistry, Pharmacy, General Anatomy, and Physiology and Surgery, and has ordered that every Candidate at an early period of his Hospital Attendance shall be individually engaged at least twice a week in the Observation and Examination of Patients, under the direction of a recognized teacher during not less than three months ; this is for the purpose of enabling him fully to profit by the Hospital instruction, and in addition to this, every Candidate is ordered, as formerly, to be also a Dresser, or to have charge of Patients equivalent to the work of a Dresser, for six months, and is also to attend demonstrations in the *post-mortem* rooms of a recognized Hospital during the whole period of Surgical Hospital practice. And to insure that these Regulations shall be carried out, the College has now instituted for the Diploma of Membership (as it had previously done for its Fellowship), a Practical Clinical Surgical Examination in addition to the Examination in Bandaging, &c., formerly instituted.

The Society of Apothecaries of London has also made some important changes. Since June, 1870, all Candidates have been required to produce evidence of having served the office of Clinical Clerk for at least six weeks, and of having been examined at the Class Examinations conducted by the teachers of the respective subjects. The Clinical Examinations which were instituted by the Society on the 13th June, 1867, have been made an integral and invariable portion of the final Examination. Students attending for their First or Primary Professional Examination have been required, since December, 1870, to undergo an Examination on Medical Regional Anatomy on the healthy subject; and in various other parts of the Examinations increased practical work has been demanded.

It is impossible to overrate the effect which the Regulations of these great Licensing Bodies (to whom the majority of English Students go for their Licences) will have on Medical Teaching in England. A great part of what was desired by the Committee of Education has been thus obtained, and it seems only just that the Council should fully recognize the improvements which have been made.

The four English Universities have made no change in their systems of Examination, which were considered satisfactory by the Council.

In Scotland the Royal College of Physicians of Edinburgh now requires all Candidates for the Licence, without exception, to undergo a Clinical Examination in Medicine in the Royal Infirmary of Edinburgh: previous to July, 1869, Students only underwent this test.

The Royal College of Surgeons of Edinburgh had, previously to July, 1869, instituted Practical Clinical Examinations, which are carried on in a Surgical Hospital, and they have since made no change in their Regulations.

The Faculty of Physicians and Surgeons of Glasgow has not essentially altered the mode of conducting the Examinations, but in some points the Examination has been more systematized, especially as regards the Clinical part. All Candidates, whether previously qualified or not, are subjected to an Examination at the bed-side, both in Medicine and Surgery. The written part of the Examination has also been extended.

The University of Edinburgh has made no alteration.

The University of Aberdeen has annulled the Regulation which exempted the Candidates who obtained the highest place in the written examination from being examined orally, and, in accordance with the wish of the Visitors from the Medical Council, enforces the oral Examination on all.

The University of Glasgow has made the Clinical Examination more efficient, but, otherwise, has made no change.

The University of St. Andrew's has made no alteration.

In Ireland the University of Dublin has improved the Clinical Examination, and now systematically enforces it on all Candidates. The previous Medical Examination (viz., in Physics, Chemistry, Botany, Materia Medica, and Descriptive Anatomy), is now compulsory.

The Queen's University in Ireland has instituted Clinical Examinations in Medicine and Surgery in the final Examination for the M.D. and Master in Surgery.

The Royal College of Surgeons of Ireland has introduced a Practical Examination in Bandaging, &c., and the Council is now engaged in the consideration of how best to introduce Clinical Examinations in Surgery.

The King and Queen's College of Physicians has instituted a Clinical Examination, which is carried on in the Wards of an Hospital for the second or final part of the Examination.

The Apothecaries' Hall of Ireland has extended the period of Examination from two to six days, so as to more practically test the Candidate's knowledge, and they have instituted a Clinical Examination of Patients, which is enforced on all Candidates.

It cannot be doubted, from the previous statements, which have been drawn from official communications received from each Licensing Body, that great progress has been made in the path indicated in the various Reports of the Visitors of the Medical Council, and of the Committee on Education.

It cannot be for a moment supposed that these alterations are made in the letter only, and are illusory. We believe that they are what they profess to be, and believing this, we must allow that the Licensing Bodies have shown a determination to improve their Curricula and Examinations, and that in several cases both are now much more efficient than formerly.

There are, however, some suggestions in the Education Report which have not yet been carried out, and on which it seems desirable the Council should express an opinion, while there are other suggestions which it will be better to keep in abeyance until the Medical Legislation, which cannot long be delayed, has been concluded.

Of the former kind, there are some of considerable importance:—

1st. The separation of the teaching of Pharmacy and Therapeutics, the former being made an early and the latter late course in the Curriculum.

The opinion of the Committee on Education, which included Dr. CHRISTISON and Dr. AQUILLA SMITH, and the views of all the best teachers of Materia Medica, were in favour of this separation. But some Licensing Bodies consider that Therapeutics should not form the subject of a separate course of study, but should be considered an essential part of the courses on practical Medicine and Surgery.

It must be admitted to be so, but still there is a necessity for special instruction, and without it, it may be confidently asserted that the progress in Therapeutics will be slow.

It seems desirable that a definite opinion should be come to on this point, and we propose to move a resolution to take the sense of the Council on this matter.

So, also, it will be for consideration how far practical instruction in drugs and pharmaceutical preparations might not be substituted for formal lectures. For the last two Sessions a plan of the kind has been carried on by Dr. HARVEY, at Aberdeen, and is said to have been highly successful.

2. The length of time assigned to Midwifery in most of the present Curricula is too short, and the Committee on Education recommended that one entire Winter Session should be assigned to this subject, and that the amount of practical instruction should be increased. This opinion was shared by all the experienced teachers in Midwifery, whose replies are given in the Appendix to the Education Report of 1869.

We therefore advise that the Council shall recommend that the systematic lectures on Midwifery shall be given in the third or fourth winter course, and that the Candidates shall be required to attend not less than 20 labours in addition to practical instruction in the diseases of women.

3. The recommendation that Pathological Anatomy shall be made a separate course has not been carried out in all cases, but several of the Licensing Bodies have endeavoured to meet it by requiring a certificate of attendance, and of practical instruction in the Dead House.

We think that a certain number of systematic lectures should be added to this practical instruction.

4. The Committee on Education strongly advised the enforcement of more regular Class Examinations. The Society of Apothecaries of London has ordered that all Students shall produce evidence of having undergone these Examinations, and we advise the Council to urge on all the Licensing Bodies to issue Regulations requiring that Written Class Examinations shall be frequent.

The other points raised in the Education Report, and which we advise should not be discussed at present, are—the length of the Sessions, the method of teaching Chemistry, and the application of Chemistry to Physiology and Pathology, the teaching of Minute Anatomy, and the definition of the areas of instruction and of examination.

The new Curricula, especially that of the College of Surgeons of England, will gradually introduce changes in some of these matters, and the probability of Parliamentary Legislation on Medical Examinations renders it now inexpedient to deal with the remaining questions.

The allusion to possible legislation leads us to the last part of the Report of the Education Committee of 1869. The Council will doubtless remember that the Committee strongly recommended the formation of conjoint Examining Boards, so as to reduce the numbers of Licences to practise from nineteen to three, and to make each Licence a Qualification in both Medicine and Surgery ; that the Council authorized circulars to the Licensing Bodies in this sense, and that in the autumn of 1869 various conferences took place between some of the Licensing Bodies, and replies were received from many of them favorable to the proposed combinations. Subsequently the action of the Government in introducing a Bill to carry out the same object suspended all negotiations of the kind.

The withdrawal of the Government measure in consequence of the opposition raised on another ground has replaced matters on the old basis.

It might indeed be argued that the willingness of the Licensing Bodies to improve their Examinations, and the fact that they really have improved them, renders it less necessary to revive the plan of a single uniform Licence to practise for each division of the Kingdom. But a moment's reflection will show that the proposal is still necessary. The independent Licences and their several Examinations still remain as numerous as ever. The competition between different bodies, therefore, still exists, and must produce its fruits, and the inequality of the Examinations in different parts of the Kingdom remains.

Any Licensing Body raising its standard beyond a certain point will certainly drive some Students, who otherwise would take its Licence, to more lenient bodies. The rigour of an Examination may then exist only on paper, and all the efforts of the Council may be spent in making ropes out of sand.

The only effectual remedy, unless the Council is prepared to be constantly inspecting and visiting the Examinations of the Licensing Bodies on a more systematic plan than heretofore, is to urge on the system of a single portal for each division of the Kingdom.

The discussions of the last two years have shown that there are no insurmountable difficulties. In England the three great Licensing Bodies have, at the instance of the Royal College of Physicians, almost arranged a scheme, and it seems to require only a little more aid to form a single Board for England. In the other divisions of the Kingdom enough has been done to show that combination can be carried out if men will earnestly try for it.

It is impossible that the Government, after introducing a Bill, should let the matter entirely drop. If it did so, the present Session has shown that there are persons ready to take the matter up ; and if the Licensing Bodies do not themselves carry out a measure of the kind, they will give great discouragement to those who desire to see them continue the representatives and guides of the Profession, but who consider the thorough Examination of those on whose skill the lives of men are to depend must be provided for at all costs.

The Council can hardly, without inconsistency, leave the Resolution of the 26th February, 1870, to remain a dead letter.

In this Resolution, which was carried by 17 votes against 1, the Council decided that it was of opinion a joint Examining Board should be formed in each division of the Kingdom. Subsequently, also, the Council passed a Resolution approving of the principles of the Medical Bill which was at that time being prepared by Lord DE GREY.

Accordingly we beg to recommend that the Council shall address a letter to each Licensing Body, transmitting a copy of the Resolution of the 26th February, 1870, and urging that arrangements for the formation of the Boards shall be undertaken without delay, so that the Council may be in a position to communicate them before the close of the year to the Government.

And we advise, in addition, that the Council shall authorize the Executive Committee to seek an interview with the Lord President of the Council, and to urge upon him the desirability of such Medical Legislation in the Session of 1872 as may carry out the object the Council proposed in passing the Resolution of February 1870, and which Lord DE GREY had in view when he introduced his Medical Bill of 1870.

(Signed)   E. A. PARKES,
Chairman.

7. *Read*—The following Letter which had been received from the Secretary of the Royal College of Surgeons of England:

ROYAL COLLEGE OF SURGEONS OF ENGLAND,
LONDON (W.C.)
23rd day of *November*, 1870.

SIR,

In pursuance of the 28th Section of the Medical Act of 1858, I am desired to acquaint you that the Council Resolved that Mr. EDWIN LOWE, lately of No. 6, George Street, Hanover Square, be removed from being a Member of this College in consequence of his having been convicted, at the Central Criminal Court, London, of felony, and sentenced to penal servitude for five years. And that they confirmed this resolution on the 13th ultimo.

I am, SIR,
Your obedient Servant,
(Signed)   EDWARD TRIMMER,
Secretary.

F. HAWKINS, Esq., M.D.

Moved by Mr. QUAIN; *Seconded* by Mr. HARGRAVE; and *Agreed to:*

> "That the name of EDWIN LOWE be removed from the *Register*."

8. A Certificate having been read of the conviction of FREDERICK HENRY MORRIS of a Misdemeanour.

Moved by Dr GULL; *Seconded* by Sir D. CORRIGAN; and *Agreed to:*

> "That the Solicitor of the Council be requested to obtain due information, and report as to the identity of FREDERICK HENRY MORRIS, convicted at Devizes, March 29th, 1871, of a Misdemeanour, with the said FREDERICK HENRY MORRIS, of Swindon, Wilts, whose name stands on the *Medical Register* for 1871."

9. *Read*—A Petition addressed to the General Medical Council by Dr. JOHN PATTISON, praying that his name may be reinstated on the *Medical Register*; with a Letter from C. H. FREWEN, Esq. (See Minutes, vol. vii., pp. 41–5.)

Moved by Dr. STOKES; *Seconded* by Dr. A. SMITH; and *Agreed to:*

> "That having heard the petition of Dr. PATTISON to be replaced on the *Register*, and having fully considered the said petition, the Council see no reason to reverse the decision to which they formerly came, after full and careful consideration of the whole case."

Moved by Dr. STORRAR; *Seconded* by Dr. SHARPEY; and *Agreed to:*

> "That the foregoing Minute be recorded."

10. *Read* — A letter from Dr. CRISP, and accompanying resolutions of a Meeting of Medical Practitioners held on 7th May, 1870.

Moved by Dr. ANDREW WOOD ; *Seconded* by Mr. HARGRAVE ; and *Agreed to :*

> "That the Registrar be directed to intimate to Dr. CRISP that his communications were received and read to the Council."

11. *Read*—A Letter from the Board of Public Examiners, Cape of Good Hope, praying that the Medical Council will be pleased to recognize their Third Class Certificate in Literature and Science, which has been assimilated to the Matriculation Examination of the London University, as fulfilling the conditions of the Council with respect to Preliminary Examinations.

Moved by Dr. BENNETT ; *Seconded* by Dr. ALEXANDER WOOD ; and *Agreed to :*

> "That the application from the Board of Public Examiners of the Cape of Good Hope be referred to a Committee to report thereon, and that Dr. GULL and Dr. STORRAR be appointed as a Committee for that purpose."

12. *Read*—A Letter addressed to the President and Medical Council, from the Honorary Secretaries of the Sydney Infirmary and Dispensary, requesting advice on the subject of founding a Medical School at Sydney, N. South Wales.

Moved by Dr. FLEMING; *Seconded* by Dr. HUMPHRY; and *Agreed to:*

"That a Letter be addressed to the Honorary Secretaries of the Sydney Infirmary and Dispensary, in reply to their request for advice on the subject of founding a Medical School in Sydney,—informing them that it is not within the province of the Medical Council to give advice on the subject; but that the Council will forward to them copies of their Reports on Medical Education."

13. *Moved* by Dr. ALEXANDER WOOD; *Seconded* by Dr. APJOHN; and *Agreed to:*

"That the returns from the Army and India Medical Boards be referred to a Committee to consider and report thereon.

The Committee to consist of:

Sir D. CORRIGAN, *Chairman.*
Dr. ALEXANDER WOOD.
Dr. ALLEN THOMSON.
Dr. APJOHN.
Mr. QUAIN.
Dr. BENNETT."

Confirmed—GEORGE EDWARD PAGET, M.D.,
President.

July 5th, 1871.

(*No.* 141.)

GENERAL COUNCIL
OF
MEDICAL EDUCATION & REGISTRATION.

MINUTES OF MEETING, WEDNESDAY, JULY 5, 1871.

32, SOHO SQUARE, LONDON, W.

Present—

Dr. PAGET, *President*, in the Chair.

Dr. BENNETT.	Dr. A. SMITH.
Mr. QUAIN.	Mr. HARGRAVE.
Dr. ACLAND.	Dr. LEET.
Dr. HUMPHRY.	Dr. APJOHN.
Dr. EMBLETON.	Sir D. CORRIGAN, Bart.
Dr. STORRAR.	Dr. PARKES.
Dr. ALEXANDER WOOD.	Dr. QUAIN.
Dr. ANDREW WOOD.	Dr. SHARPEY.
Dr. FLEMING.	Dr. GULL.
Dr. MACROBIN.	Dr. CHRISTISON.
Dr. THOMSON.	Dr. STOKES.

Dr. FRANCIS HAWKINS, *Registrar*.

The Minutes of the last Meeting were read and confirmed.

Mr. OUVRY, the Solicitor to the Council being present, Mr. WILLIAM HENRY KEMPSTER, M.R.C.S. Eng., L.S.A. Lond., L.R.C.P. Edin., appeared before the Council in pursuance of the following summons :—

To MR. WILLIAM HENRY KEMPSTER, OAK HOUSE, BATTERSEA.

A statement having been made to the General Council of Medical Education and Registration of the United Kingdom, purporting to show that you have been guilty of infamous conduct in a professional respect,* viz.: in permitting one WILLIAM GOODSON, an unqualified person, to practise under colour of your name, you sharing the profits of such practice, and to issue certificates of death, signed, or purporting to be signed, by yóu, and by which certificates it is made to appear that the deceased persons therein named were attended by you in their last illness, whereas, in truth and in fact, they were attended by the said WILLIAM GOODSON. I have to inform you that on Wednesday the 5th day of July next ensuing, at half-past two of the clock in the afternoon, the General Medical Council will meet at their office, No. 32, Soho Square, in the County of Middlesex, and will then and there institute an investigation into the truth of these allegations with a view to decide whether, upon all or any one or more of the said grounds your name ought to be removed from the *Medical Register*. At that investigation you are hereby invited and requested to be present. You will also take notice that the Meeting of this Council is fixed peremptorily for the day and hour hereinbefore named, on which day and at which hour the inquiry will be prosecuted whether you attend or not. You are further required at the time and place aforesaid to produce a certain deed or instrument, in writing, made between yourself and the said WILLIAM GOODSON, which deed was produced in evidence in a certain plaint wherein JOHN PIKE was plaintiff and the said WILLIAM GOODSON was

---

* "*Guilty of infamous conduct in a professional respect.*" (See Medical Act [1858], sec. 29.)

defendant, and which plaint was heard at the Wandsworth County Court on or about the 27th day of July, 1870. If you should neglect or refuse to produce such deed or instrument, in writing, secondary evidence of the contents thereof will be given. For your information, I give you notice that evidence will be produced in the cases of the following persons, in respect of whom death certificates signed, or purporting to be signed, by you, were given, viz. :—BENJAMIN JOHN MANLEY, who died on or about the 13th day of May, 1870; FREDERICK GEORGE WITT, who died on or about the 28th day of December, 1869; FRANCIS ANDERSON, who died on or about the 17th day of March, 1866. In mentioning these cases you must not understand that the allegations against you are, or that the evidence will be, limited to them.

Dated the first day of June, 1871.

(Signed) FRANCIS HAWKINS, M.D.,
Registrar of the General Medical Council.

Mr. OUVRY stated the case, and Mr. W. H. KEMPSTER, being called upon for his defence, stated fully to the Council his answers to the charges adduced against him, and supported them by the testimony of the following Registered Practitioners:

J. BAXTER LANGLEY, M.R.C.S. Eng.
JAMES JOSEPH, L.R.C.S. Ireland, L.K.Q.C. Phys. Ireland.
WM. GREENWOOD SUTCLIFFE, M.R.C.S. Eng., L.S.A. Lond.
WILLIAM GOODSON, L.S.A. Lond.

Moved by Dr. CHRISTISON; *Seconded* by Dr. ACLAND; and unanimously *Agreed to* :

"That the Council acquit Mr. KEMPSTER of the charges against him."

Moved by Sir D. CORRIGAN; *Seconded* by Dr. CHRISTISON; and *Agreed to:*

> "That the facts which have come to the knowledge of the General Medical Council in the investigation of the case of Mr. W. H. KEMPSTER have impressed this Council with the conviction that an amendment of the laws in force in regard to Death Registry is most urgently required; and that a copy of this Resolution be forwarded to the Secretary of State for the Home Department."

Confirmed—GEORGE EDWARD PAGET, M.D.,
President.

July 6th, 1871.

(*No.* 142.)

GENERAL COUNCIL
OF
MEDICAL EDUCATION & REGISTRATION.

MINUTES OF MEETING, THURSDAY, JULY 6, 1871.

32, SOHO SQUARE, LONDON, W.

Present—

Dr. PAGET, *President*, in the Chair.

Dr. BENNETT.	Dr. A. SMITH.
Mr. QUAIN.	Mr. HARGRAVE.
Dr. ACLAND.	Dr. LEET.
Dr. HUMPHRY.	Dr. APJOHN.
Dr. EMBLETON.	Sir D. CORRIGAN, Bart.
Dr. STORRAR.	Dr. PARKES.
Dr. ALEXANDER WOOD.	Dr. QUAIN.
Dr. ANDREW WOOD.	Dr. SHARPEY.
Dr. FLEMING.	Dr. GULL.
Dr. MACROBIN.	Dr. CHRISTISON.
Dr. THOMSON.	Dr. STOKES.

Dr. FRANCIS HAWKINS, *Registrar*.

The Minutes of the last Meeting were read and confirmed.

1. *Moved* by Dr. STORRAR; *Seconded* by Dr. GULL; and *Agreed to :*

"That the Education Report (*see* Minutes, Vol. ix. pp. 7-13) be taken as read."

2. *Moved* by Dr. PARKES and *Seconded* by Dr. CHRISTISON:

I. "That it is desirable that the instruction in Pharmacy should be separated from that in Therapeutics, and that the former should be obtained at an early, and the latter at a later period of the Professional Curriculum."

Amendment, *Moved* by Dr. HUMPHRY and *Seconded* by Dr. APJOHN:

"That practical instruction in Pharmacy may with advantage be substituted for formal Lectures on the Subject, and should be attended at an early period of the Medical Curriculum; and that instruction in Therapeutics should be conducted at a later period of the Professional Curriculum, either by a special Course of Lectures, or as an essential part of the Courses of Lectures on Medicine and Surgery."

The Amendment was *Negatived.*

The Motion was then put to the Vote and *Carried.*

3. *Moved* by Dr. PARKES and *Seconded* by Mr. HARGRAVE:

"That it is desirable that the Course on Midwifery should be extended, and that every Candidate for a Licence shall be required to attend not less than 20 labours."

Amendment, *Moved* by Dr. MACROBIN and *Seconded* by Dr. ANDREW WOOD :

"That it is desirable that instruction in Midwifery should be extended beyond three months, so as to embrace instruction in the Diseases of Women and Children, and that every Candidate for a Licence should be required to attend not less than 10 cases of labour."

The Amendment was *Negatived*.

Amendment, *Moved* by Dr. ANDREW WOOD and *Seconded* by Dr. MACROBIN :

"That it is desirable that the instruction in Midwifery should be extended, and that every Candidate for a Licence should be required to attend not less than 10 labours."

The Amendment was *Negatived*.

The original Motion was then put to the Vote, and also *Negatived*.

4. *Moved* by Dr. PARKES and *Seconded* by Dr. ANDREW WOOD:

"That it is desirable that instruction in Pathological Anatomy should include a certain number of Systematic Lectures."

Amendment, *Moved* by Dr. HUMPHRY and *Seconded* by Dr. STOKES:

"That it is desirable that systematic instruction in Pathological Anatomy should form a part of Professional Education."

The Amendment was *Carried*, and having been put as a Substantive Motion, was also *Carried*.

5. *Moved* by Dr. PARKES and *Seconded* by Dr HUMPHRY:

"That it is desirable that Class Examinations should be compulsory, and that the Licensing Bodies should require them in all cases."

Amendment, *Moved* by Sir D. CORRIGAN and *Seconded* by Dr. A. SMITH:

"That it is desirable that Class Examinations should form a part of every Course of Lectures, whether systematic or Clinical."

The Amendment was *Negatived*.

Amendment, *Moved* by Dr. ACLAND and *Seconded* by Mr. QUAIN:

"That it is desirable that Class Examinations should be compulsory on Students."

The Amendment was *Negatived*.

Amendment, *Moved* by Mr. QUAIN and *Seconded* by Dr. A. SMITH:

"That it is desirable that Class Examinations should form a necessary part of every Course of Instruction."

The Amendment was *Carried*, and having been put as a Substantive Motion, was also *Carried*.

Confirmed—GEORGE EDWARD PAGET, M.D.,
President.

July 7th, 1871.

(*No.* 143.)

GENERAL COUNCIL
OF
MEDICAL EDUCATION & REGISTRATION.

MINUTES OF MEETING, FRIDAY, JULY 7, 1871.

32, SOHO SQUARE, LONDON, W.

Present—
Dr. PAGET, *President,* in the Chair.

Dr. BENNETT.	Dr. A. SMITH.
Mr. QUAIN.	Mr. HARGRAVE.
Dr. ACLAND.	Dr. LEET.
Dr. HUMPHRY.	Dr. APJOHN.
Dr. EMBLETON.	Sir D. CORRIGAN, Bart.
Dr. STORRAR.	Dr. PARKES.
Dr. ALEXANDER WOOD.	Dr. QUAIN.
Dr. ANDREW WOOD.	Dr. SHARPEY.
Dr. FLEMING.	Dr. GULL.
Dr. MACROBIN.	Dr. CHRISTISON.
Dr. THOMSON.	Dr. STOKES.

Dr. FRANCIS HAWKINS, *Registrar.*

The Minutes of the last Meeting were read and confirmed.

1. *Moved* by Dr. ACLAND; *Seconded* by Dr. ANDREW WOOD; and *Agreed to :*

> "That Dr. BENNETT's Statement, of which notice had been given, take precedence of other Business."

By permission of the Council, Dr. BENNETT made a Statement in reference to arrangements for a Conjoint Examining Board for England, agreed to by a Conjoint Committee of the Royal Colleges of Physicians and Surgeons of England.

2. *Moved* by Dr. FLEMING and *Seconded* by Dr. MACROBIN:

> "That it is desirable that Clinical Instruction in Medicine and in Surgery should not be conducted so much by formal Lectures in Class Rooms as appears from the evidence before the Council to be the case at present; but that Hospital Students should be divided into Classes of limited numbers, so as to enable them individually to observe cases of disease, and to be examined upon them conversationally at the bed-side or in proximity to it. Further, that it is desirable that, where possible, all Students should serve as Clinical Assistants or Dressers."

Amendment, *Moved* by Dr. GULL and *Seconded* by Dr. STOKES:

> "That the Council express their sense of the importance of making Clinical Instruction year by year more practical, and more conversant with the phenomena of Disease, and less dependent upon formal Clinical Lectures."

The Amendment was *Negatived*.

The Motion was then put to the Vote, and also *Negatived*.

3. *Moved* by Dr. STORRAR and *Seconded* by Mr. QUAIN:

"That it is desirable that Students should have the option of acquiring an adequate knowledge of Chemistry, and of passing an Examination in it, before they enter upon the period recognized by the Licensing Bodies as the Course of Professional Study."

Amendment, *Moved* by Dr. APJOHN and *Seconded* by Dr. ANDREW WOOD:

"That Chemistry is a most important branch of Medical Education, and that the Council does not think it desirable to adopt any Resolution which, if it had any practical effect, would tend to discourage the efficient study of the subject by Medical Students."

The Amendment was *Negatived*.

The Original Motion was then put to the Vote, and also *Negatived*.

4. *Moved* by Dr. PARKES; *Seconded* by Dr. STORRAR; and *Agreed to*:

"That a Letter be addressed to each Licensing Body transmitting a copy of the Resolution of the Council of the 26th February, 1870 (*see* Vol. viii., pp. 32-4), on the formation of Conjoint Examining Boards, and urging that arrangements for the formation of such Boards should be undertaken without delay, and should be communicated to the President of this Council before the close of the present year."

Dr. STORRAR required that the names and numbers of those who Voted for the Motion, and of those who declined to Vote, should be taken down.

For, 21.

THE PRESIDENT.
Dr. BENNETT.
Mr. QUAIN.
Dr. HUMPHRY.
Dr. EMBLETON.
Dr. STORRAR.
Dr. ALEXANDER WOOD.
Dr. ANDREW WOOD.
Dr. FLEMING.
Dr. MACROBIN.
Dr. THOMSON.
Dr. SMITH.
Mr. HARGRAVE.
Dr. LEET.
Dr. APJOHN.
Dr. SHARPEY.
Dr. PARKES.
Dr. QUAIN.
Dr. GULL.
Dr. CHRISTISON.
Dr. STOKES.

Declined to Vote :—

Sir D. CORRIGAN, Bart.

Two Members of the Council were absent.

RESOLUTION OF THE 26TH FEBRUARY, 1870.

"That this Council is of opinion that a Joint Examining Board should be formed in each of the Three Divisions of the Kingdom, and that every person who desires to be Registered under any of the Qualifications recognised in Schedule (A) to the Medical Act, shall be required, previously to such Registration, to appear before one of these Boards, and be Examined on all the Subjects which may be deemed advisable by the Medical Council; the rights and privileges of the Universities and Corporations being left, in all other respects, the same as at present."

5. *Moved* by Dr. PARKES; *Seconded* by Dr. ANDREW WOOD; and *Agreed to*:

"That the first Resolution of the 28th February, 1870, (*see* Vol. viii, p. 37) be also transmitted to the Licensing Bodies at the same time as the previous Resolution."

RESOLUTION OF 28TH FEBRUARY, 1870.

"That in accordance with the foregoing Resolution (*see* Vol. viii, p. 32, Sect. 2), the Universities and Medical Corporations established in each division of the United Kingdom, shall be requested to concert a Scheme for the constitution and regulation of a Conjoint Examining Board for that part of the Kingdom to which they belong, and shall, on or before June 1, 1870, transmit such Scheme to the consideration of the General Medical Council."

6. *Moved* by Dr. ANDREW WOOD; *Seconded* by Mr. HARGRAVE; and *Agreed to*:

"That the Report of the Committee on Education be recommitted, and brought up to-morrow in a form adapted to the Resolutions of the Council."

Confirmed—GEORGE EDWARD PAGET, M.D.,
President.

July 8th, 1871.

(No. 144.)

GENERAL COUNCIL
OF
MEDICAL EDUCATION & REGISTRATION.

MINUTES OF MEETING, SATURDAY, JULY 8, 1871

32, Soho Square, London, W.

Present—

Dr. PAGET, *President*, in the Chair.

Dr. BENNETT.	Dr. A. SMITH.
Mr. QUAIN.	Mr. HARGRAVE.
Dr. ACLAND.	Dr. LEET.
Dr. HUMPHRY.	Dr. APJOHN.
Dr. EMBLETON.	Sir D. CORRIGAN, Bart.
Dr. STORRAR.	Dr. PARKES.
Dr. ALEXANDER WOOD.	Dr. QUAIN.
Dr. ANDREW WOOD.	Dr. SHARPEY.
Dr. FLEMING.	Dr. GULL.
Dr. MACROBIN.	Dr. CHRISTISON.
Dr. THOMSON.	Dr. STOKES.

Dr. FRANCIS HAWKINS, *Registrar*.

The Minutes of the last Meeting were read and confirmed.

1. *Moved* by Dr. ANDREW WOOD; *Seconded* by Sir D. CORRIGAN; and *Agreed to*:

> "That the Registrar be directed to erase from the *Register* the name of FREDERICK HENRY MORRIS, of Swindon, Wilts, the Council being satisfied that he is the same person who was convicted at Devizes, on the 27th day of March, 1871, of a Misdemeanour, and of whose conviction a legal certificate has been submitted to the Council."

2. *Moved* by Dr. STORRAR; *Seconded* by Dr. PARKES; and *Agreed to*:

> "That the Report of the Committee on the application from the Board of Public Examiners of the Cape of Good Hope, be received and adopted."

REPORT.

The Committee find that the Board of Public Examiners in Literature and Science, Cape of Good Hope, is constituted under an Act of the Legislature of the Colony.

The Examination Papers for the Third Class Certificates referred to show that the Examinations, as stated, correspond generally with the Matriculation Examination at the University of London. The Committee therefore advise the Council to recognize these Certificates as fulfilling the conditions of the Preliminary Examination.

(Signed)   WILLIAM W. GULL.
                 JOHN STORRAR.

July 5, 1871.

3. The Council having balloted for the Executive Committee the following were found to be elected:

> Dr. BENNETT.
> Dr. ACLAND.
> Dr. SHARPEY.
> Dr. QUAIN.
> Dr. ANDREW WOOD.
> Dr. A. SMITH.

4. *Moved* by Dr. BENNETT and *Seconded* by Dr. THOMSON.

> "That it be referred to the Executive Committee to Report on the most desirable mode of procedure in the case of Motions having reference to any Penal Measures."

The Motion was *Agreed to.*

5. *Read*—The following Report of the Finance Committee.

REPORT.

The Finance Committee beg leave to present, in the Table subjoined, a Statement of the Income and Expenditure of the year 1870, compared with the Income and Expenditure of the preceding year, also an Estimate for 1871.

It will be seen that there has been an increase of income in 1870, and that this is partly due to an increase in the number of Registration fees; but it includes also the balance of the Pharmacopœia Account and the proceeds of sales, making together £607 6s., which, by direction of the Council, is now included in the ordinary income. The debt still owing to the Council on account of the Pharmacopœia was reduced in January last to £104 14s.

The expenditure of 1870 is less by £302 13s. 8d. than that of 1869. The reduction is to a considerable extent due to a diminished charge for Printing, especially for printing Reports of Committees. It is expected that a considerable permanent saving under this head of expense will be effected by an arrangement that has been entered into for printing and binding the *Medical Register* at a reduced cost through the agency of Her Majesty's Stationery Office.

(Signed)   W. SHARPEY,

Chairman.

	Actual Income for the Year 1869.			Actual Income for the Year 1870.			Estimated Income for the Year 1871.		
	£	s.	d.	£	s.	d.	£	s.	d.
Fees received by—									
Branch Council for England	2281	15	0	2358	0	0	2377	16	8
,, ,, Scotland	617	10	0	725	0	0	699	16	8
,, ,, Ireland	732	0	0	1047	5	0	872	6	8
			3631 5 0			4130 5 0			3950 0 0
Dividends received by—									
Branch Council for England	644	18	9	677	1	3	670	0	0
,, ,, Scotland	64	10	10	68	2	2	65	0	0
,, ,, Ireland	64	2	0	65	19	5	60	0	0
Sale of Registers	773	11	7	270	10	0	270	0	0
Sale of Pharmacopœias and Balance of Account	271	7	6	607	6	0	200	0	0
Penalties	47	14	6	9	19	0	470	0	0
			887 15 0						
			£4723 18 7			£5829 2 10			£5215 0 0

	Actual Expenditure for the Year 1869.			Actual Expenditure for the Year 1870.			Estimated Expenditure for the Year 1871.		
	£	s.	d.	£	s.	d.	£	s.	d.
Expenses of—									
General Council			4265 13 9			4060 11 9			4000 0 0
Branch Council for England	642	9	10	597	18	9	642	0	0
,, ,, Scotland	286	0	7	240	13	0	286	0	0
,, ,, Ireland	295	9	10	287	16	10	295	0	0
			1224 0 3			1126 8 7			1223 0 0
Total Expenditure			5489 14 0			5187 0 4	Estimated Total Expenditure		5223 0 0
Total Income			4723 18 7	Actual Income		5829 2 10	Estimated Total Income		5215 0 0
Excess of Expenditure over Income			£765 15 5	Balance in favour of Council		£642 2 6	Excess of Expenditure over Income		£8 0 0

Moved by Dr. SHARPEY; *Seconded* by Dr. STORRAR; and *Agreed to:*

"That the Report of the Finance Committee be received and adopted."

6. Dr. SHARPEY having signified his desire to resign the office of Treasurer of the General Medical Council, the PRESIDENT proposed, and it was assented to by *acclamation:*

"That the hearty thanks of the Council be returned to Dr. SHARPEY for his long and valuable services as Treasurer."

Moved by Dr. SMITH; *Seconded* by Dr. PARKES; and *Agreed to:*

"That Dr. BENNETT be elected Treasurer of the General Medical Council."

7. *Read*—The following Report of the Committee on the Returns from the Army and Indian Medical Boards:

REPORT.

The Committee appointed July 4th to consider and report on the Returns from the Army and Indian Medical Boards, recommend that the following communications be addressed to The Director-General of the Army Medical Department, and to the Major-General, Military Secretary, India Office:

To THE DIRECTOR-GENERAL, ARMY MEDICAL DEPARTMENT.

SIR,
I am directed by the General Medical Council to thank you for the statement with which you have favoured them, "of the Degrees, Diplomas, and Licences of the Candidates for Commissions in the Medical Department of the Army, who in February last presented themselves for Examination," and to ask you, should you see no objection, to make a slight alteration in the last column, which, although sufficiently intelligible to a careful reader, might be misunderstood by some.

The alteration I am directed to suggest is, that in future Returns the last column headed "Candidates" should stand thus, as may be illustrated by applying it to the present Return—

"Total No. of Candidates 57

Succeeded in obtaining Appointments . . . 36
Succeeded in Examination, but not in obtaining Appointments, there being only 36 Vacancies } 17
Failed in Examination 4

Total . . 57 "

To THE MAJOR-GENERAL, MILITARY SECRETARY, INDIA OFFICE.

SIR,

I am directed by the General Medical Council to thank you for the statement with which you have favoured them, "of the Degrees, Diplomas, and Licences of the Candidates in the Medical Department of the Indian Army, who, in February 1870, presented themselves for Examination at Chelsea Hospital;" and to ask you, should you see no objection, to make a slight alteration in the last column, which, although sufficiently intelligible to a careful reader, might be misunderstood by some.

The alteration I am directed to suggest is, that in future Returns, the last column, headed "Candidates," should stand thus; as may be illustrated by applying it to the present Return—

"Total No. of Candidates 23

Succeeded in obtaining Appointments . . 10
Succeeded in Examination but not in obtaining Appointments, there being only 10 Vacancies 9
Failed in Examination 4

Total . 23 "

(Signed) D. CORRIGAN,

Chairman.

Moved by Sir D. CORRIGAN; *Seconded* by Dr. PARKES; and *Agreed to*:

"That the preceding Report be received and adopted, and that the letters drafted therein be signed by the Registrar, and forwarded by him as directed."

8. *Read*—The following Report of the Pharmacopœia Committee:

REPORT.

The Pharmacopœia Committee appointed by Minute of the Council, July 12, 1869, beg to report that, owing to the pressure of important business during the Sessions of the Council last year, no Meeting of the Committee was held, and no Report was prepared for their consideration by Dr. REDWOOD.

The Committee met on the 7th instant, and received a Report from Dr. REDWOOD, on the progress of Pharmacy since the date of his last Report. Some points of importance in connection with Pharmaceutical preparations were discussed, and Dr. REDWOOD was requested to continue his services. It was also resolved that Dr. CHRISTISON, Dr. QUAIN, and Dr. AQUILLA SMITH be requested to continue their inquiries as regards additions or other changes in the Pharmacopœia, and that Dr. REDWOOD be requested, in addition to his duty of reporting on the progress of Pharmacy, to investigate, from time to time, the composition of articles in the Pharmacopœia, concerning which questions have been raised.

As the sum of £75 remains as balance in the hands of the Committee, it will be unnecessary to ask the Council to place any further sum at the disposal of the Committee for use during the ensuing year.

(Signed) R. CHRISTISON,

Chairman.

July 7th, 1871.

Moved by Dr. CHRISTISON; *Seconded* by Dr. QUAIN; and *Agreed to:*

"That the Report of the Pharmacopœia Committee be received and adopted."

Moved by Dr. BENNETT; *Seconded* by Dr. PARKES; and *Agreed to:*

"That the Pharmacopœia Committee of last year, consisting of
- Dr. CHRISTISON.
- Dr. QUAIN.
- Dr. SHARPEY.
- Dr. A. SMITH.

be reappointed."

10. *Moved* by Dr. ALEXANDER WOOD; *Seconded* by Dr. HUMPHRY; and *Agreed to:*

"That it is desirable that the Visitation of the Preliminary Examinations and of those of the Licensing Boards be recommenced, and that a Committee be appointed to consider the best means of doing so."

The Committee to consist of:
- Dr. ALEXANDER WOOD, *Chairman.*
- Dr. HUMPHRY.
- Dr. THOMSON.
- Mr. QUAIN.
- Dr. A. SMITH.
- Dr. SHARPEY.
- Dr. STORRAR.

Confirmed—GEORGE EDWARD PAGET, M.D.,
President.

July 10*th*, 1871.

(*No.* 145.)

GENERAL COUNCIL
OF
MEDICAL EDUCATION & REGISTRATION.

MINUTES OF MEETING, MONDAY, JULY 10, 1871.

32, Soho Square, London, W.

Present—

Dr. Paget, *President*, in the Chair.

Dr. Bennett.	Dr. A. Smith.
Mr. Quain.	Mr. Hargrave.
Dr. Acland.	Dr. Leet.
Dr. Humphry.	Dr. Apjohn.
Dr. Embleton.	Sir D. Corrigan, Bart.
Dr. Storrar.	Dr. Parkes.
Dr. Alexander Wood.	Dr. Quain.
Dr. Andrew Wood.	Dr. Sharpey.
Dr. Fleming.	Dr. Gull.
Dr. Macrobin.	Dr. Stokes.
Dr. Thomson.	

Dr. Francis Hawkins, *Registrar*.

The Minutes of the last Meeting were read and confirmed.

1. *Read*—The following Amended Report of the Committee on Professional Education:

AMENDED REPORT OF THE EDUCATION COMMITTEE.

THE Report of the Committee of 1869 on Professional Education, and the replies to the letter of the Chairman from Teachers on Medical Education, were forwarded to the Licensing Bodies, and answers were received from them in 1870.

All the answers did not arrive in time to be presented at the meetings of Council in 1870, and accordingly an *interim* report only was then laid before the Council (Minutes, Vol. viii. p. 11). By a resolution of Council (Minutes, Vol. viii. p. 105), the Committee on Education was reappointed, and directed to report at a future meeting of the Council.

Subsequently replies to the first Education Report having been received from all the Licensing Bodies, they were printed and distributed, last autumn, to the Members of Council, and are contained in the Appendix to the 8th Volume of the Minutes of the Meetings of the Council.

The probability that an Act to regulate Medical Education would be passed in 1870, rendered it inexpedient to discuss last year many of the suggestions contained in the Education Report, and in the replies sent in by the Licensing Bodies, for if the Medical Bill of 1870 had been passed, it would have necessitated a revision of the whole subject of Medical Education and Examination, and would have rendered any previous decisions null and void.

During the last two years very important alterations have been made in the system of Education and Examination by some of the Licensing Bodies, and several of the suggestions of the Education Committee have been met.

The Royal College of Physicians of London, by a rule passed in April 1871, requires from every Candidate for its Licence, evidence that he has discharged the duties of Clinical Clerk, and of Dresser, for periods of three months respectively, and thus one important recommendation of the Education Report has been carried out.

The Royal College of Surgeons of England, on the reception of the Report, appointed a Committee to consider it, and eventually determined to act on the opinion of their Court of Examiners of the 16th December, 1869, that "every part of the knowledge included in, or accessory to, the Education of Candidates for the Diplomas of the College ought to be taught and learnt practically." The College has, therefore, introduced into its Curriculum clauses which insure practical instruction in Chemistry, Pharmacy, General Anatomy and Physiology, and Surgery, and has ordered that every Candidate at an early period of his Hospital Attendance shall be individually engaged at least twice a week in the Observation and Examination of Patients, under the direction of a recognized teacher during not less than three months; this is for the purpose of enabling him fully to profit by the Hospital instruction, and in addition to this, every Candidate is ordered, as formerly, to be also a Dresser, or to have charge of Patients equivalent to the work of a Dresser, for six months, and is also to attend demonstrations in the *post-mortem* rooms of a recognized Hospital during the whole period of Surgical Hospital practice. And to insure that these Regulations shall be carried out, the College has now instituted for the Diploma of Membership (as it had previously done for its Fellowship), a Practical Clinical Surgical Examination in addition to the Examination in Bandaging, &c., formerly instituted.

The Society of Apothecaries of London has also made some important changes. Since June 1870, all Candidates have been required to produce evidence of having served the office of Clinical Clerk for at least six weeks, and of having been examined at the Class Examinations conducted by the teachers of the respective subjects. The Clinical Examinations which were instituted by the Society on the 13th June, 1867, have been made an integral and invariable portion of the final Examination. Students attending for their First or Primary Professional Examination have been required, since December 1870, to undergo an Examination on Medical Regional Anatomy on the healthy subject; and in various other parts of the Examinations increased practical work has been demanded.

It is impossible to overrate the effect which the Regulations of these great Licensing Bodies (to whom the majority of English Students go for their Licences) will have on Medical Teaching in England. A great part of what was desired by the Committee of Education has been thus obtained, and it seems only just that the Council should fully recognize the improvements which have been made.

The four English Universities have made no change in their systems of Examination, which were considered satisfactory by the Council.

In Scotland the Royal College of Physicians of Edinburgh now requires all Candidates for the Licence, without exception, to undergo a Clinical Examination in Medicine in the Royal Infirmary of Edinburgh : previous to July 1869, Students only underwent this test.

The Royal College of Surgeons of Edinburgh had, previously to July 1869, instituted Practical Clinical Examinations, which are carried on in a Surgical Hospital, and they have since made no change in their Regulations.

The Faculty of Physicians and Surgeons of Glasgow has not essentially altered the mode of conducting the Examinations, but in some points the Examination has been more systematized, especially as regards the Clinical part. All Candidates, whether previously qualified or not, are subjected to an Examination at the bed-side, both in Medicine and Surgery. The written part of the Examination has also been extended.

The University of Edinburgh has made no alteration.

Practical Study, and Class Examinations in all branches of Medical Education, Clinical Examinations of the Students in Medicine, Clinical Examinations of Candidates both in Surgery and Medicine, were in force for some time previous to the Report of this Committee in 1869; and the University contemplate the requirement of Study as Clinical Clerks and Dressers, so soon as the General Council report in favour of that measure.

The University of Aberdeen has annulled the Regulation which exempted the Candidates who obtained the highest place in the written Examination from being examined orally, and, in accordance with the wish of the Visitors from the Medical Council, enforces the oral Examination on all.

The University of Glasgow has made the Clinical Examination more efficient, but, otherwise, has made no change.

The University of St. Andrew's has made no alteration.

In Ireland the University of Dublin has improved the Clinical Examination, and now systematically enforces it on all Candidates. The previous Medical Examination (viz., in Physics, Chemistry, Botany, Materia Medica, and Descriptive Anatomy), is now compulsory.

The Queen's University in Ireland has instituted Clinical Examinations in Medicine and Surgery in the final Examination for the M.D. and Master in Surgery.

The Royal College of Surgeons of Ireland had formerly instituted a Practical Examination in Bandaging, &c., and the Council has now ordered Clinical Examinations in Surgery and in Medicine for the final Examination.

The King and Queen's College of Physicians has instituted a Clinical Examination, which is carried on in the Wards of an Hospital for the second or final part of the Examination.

The Apothecaries' Hall of Ireland has extended the period of Examination from two to six days, so as to more practically test the Candidate's knowledge, and they have instituted a Clinical Examination of Patients which is enforced on all Candidates.

It cannot be doubted, from the previous statements, which have been drawn from official communications received from each Licensing Body, that great progress has been made in the path indicated in the various Reports of the Visitors of the Medical Council, and of the Committee on Education.

There are, however, some suggestions in the Education Report which have not yet been carried out, and on which it seems desirable the Council should express an opinion, while there are other suggestions which it will be better to keep in abeyance.

Of the former kind, there are some of considerable importance :—

1st. The separation of the teaching of Pharmacy and Therapeutics, the former being made an early, and the latter a late course in the Curriculum.

The opinion of the Committee on Education, which included Dr. CHRISTISON and Dr. AQUILLA SMITH, and the views of all the best teachers of Materia

Medica, were in favour of this separation. But some Licensing Bodies consider that Therapeutics should not form the subject of a separate course of study, but should be considered an essential part of the courses on practical Medicine and Surgery.

It must be admitted to be so, but still there is a necessity for special instruction, and without it, it may be confidently asserted that the progress in Therapeutics will be slow.

It seems desirable that a definite opinion should be come to on this point, that the Instruction in Pharmacy should be separated from that in Therapeutics, and that the former should be obtained at an early, and the latter at a later period of the Professional Curriculum.

So, also, it will be for consideration how far practical instruction in drugs and pharmaceutical preparations might not be substituted for formal lectures. For the last two Sessions a plan of the kind has been carried on by Dr. HARVEY, at Aberdeen, and is said to have been highly successful.

2. The recommendation that Pathological Anatomy should be made a separate course has not been carried out in all cases, but several of the Licensing Bodies have endeavoured to meet it by requiring a certificate of attendance, and of practical instruction in the Dead House.

It is desirable that systematic instruction in Pathological Anatomy should form a part of Professional Education.

3. The Committee on Education strongly advised the enforcement of more regular Class Examinations. The Society of Apothecaries' of London has ordered that all Students shall produce evidence of having undergone these Examinations, and it is desirable that all the Licensing Bodies should issue Regulations that Class Examinations shall form a necessary part of every course of instruction.

The other points raised in the Education Report of 1869, and which we advise should not be discussed at present, are—the length of the Sessions, the method of teaching Chemistry, and the application of Chemistry to Physiology and Pathology, the teaching of Minute Anatomy, and the definition of the areas of Instruction and of Examination.

The Council will doubtless remember that the Education Report of 1869 strongly recommended the formation of conjoint Examining Boards, so as to reduce the number of Licences to practise from nineteen to three, and to make each Licence a Qualification in both Medicine and Surgery; that the Council authorized circulars to the Licensing Bodies on this sense, and that in the autumn of 1869 various conferences took place between some of the Licensing Bodies, and replies were received from many of them favourable to the proposed combinations. Subsequently the action of the Government in introducing a Bill to carry out the same object, suspended all negotiations of the kind.

The withdrawal of the Government measure in consequence of the opposition on another ground has replaced matters on the old basis.

It might indeed be argued that the willingness of the Licensing Bodies to improve their Examinations, and the fact that they really have improved them, renders it less necessary to revive the plan of a single uniform Licence to practise for each division of the Kingdom. But a moment's reflection will show that the proposal is still necessary. The independent Licences and their several Examinations still remain as numerous as ever. The competition between different bodies, therefore, still exists, and must produce its fruits, and the inequality of the Examinations in different parts of the Kingdom remains.

The only effectual remedy, unless the Council is prepared to be constantly inspecting and visiting the Examinations of the Licensing Bodies on a more systematic plan than heretofore, is to urge on the system of a single portal for each division of the Kingdom.

The discussions of the last two years have shown that there are no insurmountable difficulties. In England the principal Licensing Bodies have, at the instance of the Royal College of Physicians, almost arranged a scheme, and it seems to require only a little more aid to form a single Board for England. In the other divisions of the Kingdom enough has been done to show that combination can be carried out if men will earnestly try for it.

It is impossible that the Government, after introducing a Bill, should let the matter entirely drop. If it did so, the present Session has shown that there are persons ready to take the matter up; and if the Licensing Bodies do not themselves carry out a measure of the kind, they will give great discouragement to those who desire to see them continue the representatives and guides of the Profession, but who consider the thorough Examination of those on whose skill the lives of men are to depend must be provided for at all costs.

The Council can hardly, without inconsistency, leave the Resolution of the 26th February, 1870, to remain a dead letter.

In this Resolution, which was carried by 17 votes against 1, the Council decided that it was of opinion a joint Examining Board should be formed in each division of the Kingdom. Subsequently, also, the Council passed a Resolution approving of the principles of the Medical Bill which was at that time being prepared by LORD DE GREY.

It is, therefore, desirable that the Council should address a letter to each Licensing Body, transmitting a copy of the Resolution of the 26th February, 1870, and urging that arrangements for the formation of the Boards shall be undertaken without delay.

(Signed) E. A. PARKES,
Chairman.

The Report was then fully considered by the Council in Committee, and further amended as follows:

AMENDED REPORT OF THE COMMITTEE ON PROFESSIONAL EDUCATION.

THE Report of the Committee of 1869 on Professional Education, and the replies to the letter of the Chairman from Teachers on Medical Education, were forwarded to the Licensing Bodies, and answers were received from them in 1870.

All the answers did not arrive in time to be presented at the meetings of Council in 1870, and accordingly an *interim* report only was then laid before the Council (Minutes, Vol. viii. p. 11). By a resolution of Council (Minutes, Vol. viii. p. 105), the Committee on Education was reappointed, and directed to report at a future meeting of the Council.

Subsequently replies to the first Education Report having been received from all the Licensing Bodies, they were printed and distributed, last autumn, to the Members of Council, and are contained in the Appendix to the 8th Volume of the Minutes of the Meetings of the Council.

The probability that an Act to regulate Medical Education would be passed in 1870, rendered it inexpedient to discuss last year many of the suggestions contained in the Education Report, and in the replies sent in by the Licensing Bodies, for if the Medical Bill of 1870 had been passed, it would have necessitated a revision of the whole subject of Medical Education and Examination, and would have rendered any previous decisions null and void.

During the last two years very important alterations have been made in the system of Education and Examination by some of the Licensing Bodies, and several of the suggestions of the Education Committee have been met.

The Royal College of Physicians of London, by a rule passed in April, 1871, requires from every Candidate for its Licence, evidence that he has discharged the duties of Clinical Clerk, and of Dresser, for periods of three months respectively, and thus one important recommendation of the Education Report has been carried out.

The Royal College of Surgeons of England, on the reception of the Report, appointed a Committee to consider it, and eventually determined to act on the opinion of their Court of Examiners of the 16th December, 1869, that "every part of the knowledge included in, or accessory to, the Education of Candidates for the Diplomas of the College ought to be taught and learnt practically." The College has, therefore, introduced into its Curriculum clauses which insure practical instruction in Chemistry, Pharmacy, General Anatomy and Physiology, and Surgery, and has ordered that every Candidate at an early period of his Hospital Attendance shall be individually engaged at least twice a week in the Observation and Examination of Patients, under the direction of a recognized teacher during not less than three months; this is for the purpose of enabling him fully to profit by the Hospital instruction, and in addition to this, every Candidate is ordered, as formerly, to be also a Dresser, or to have charge of Patients equivalent to the work of a Dresser, for six months, and is also to attend demonstrations in the *post-mortem* rooms of a recognized Hospital during the whole period of Surgical Hospital practice. To insure that these Regulations shall be carried out, the College has now instituted for the Diploma of Membership (as it had previously done for its Fellowship), a Practical Clinical Surgical Examination in addition to the Examination in Bandaging, &c., formerly instituted.

The Society of Apothecaries of London has also made some important changes. Since June 1870, all Candidates have been required to produce evidence of having served the office of Clinical Clerk for at least six weeks, and of having been examined at the Class Examinations conducted by the teachers of the respective subjects. The Clinical Examinations which were instituted by the Society on the 13th June, 1867, have been made an integral and invariable portion of the final Examination. Students attending for their First or Primary Professional Examination have been required, since December 1870, to undergo an Examination on Medical Regional Anatomy on the healthy subject; and in various other parts of the Examinations increased practical work has been demanded.

It is impossible to overrate the effect which the Regulations of these great Licensing Bodies (to whom the majority of English Students go for their Licences) will have on Medical Teaching in England. A great part of what was desired by the Committee of Education has been thus obtained, and it seems only just that the Council should fully recognize the improvements which have been made.

The four English Universities have made no change in their systems of Examination.

In Scotland the Royal College of Physicians of Edinburgh now requires all Candidates for the Licence, without exception, to undergo a Clinical Examination in Medicine in the Royal Infirmary of Edinburgh.

The Royal College of Surgeons of Edinburgh had, previous to July 1869, instituted Practical Clinical Examinations, which are carried on in a Surgical Hospital, and they have since made no change in their Regulations.

The Faculty of Physicians and Surgeons of Glasgow has not essentially altered the mode of conducting the Examinations, but in some points the Examination has been more systematized, especially as regards the Clinical part. All Candidates, whether previously qualified or not, are subjected to an Examination at the bed-side, both in Medicine and Surgery. The written part of the Examination has also been extended.

The University of Edinburgh has made no alteration. Practical Study, and Class Examinations in all branches of Medical Education, Clinical Examinations of the Students in Medicine, Clinical Examinations of Candidates both in Surgery and Medicine, were in force for some time previous to the Report of the Education Committee of 1869; and the University contemplates the requirement of Study as Clinical Clerks and Dressers, so soon as the General Council report in favour of that measure.

The University of Aberdeen has annulled the Regulation which exempted the Candidates who obtained the highest place in the written Examination from being examined orally, and, in accordance with the wish of the Visitors from the Medical Council, enforce the oral Examination on all.

The University of Glasgow has made the Clinical Examinations more efficient, but otherwise has made no change.

The University of St. Andrew's has made no alteration.

In Ireland the University of Dublin has improved the Clinical Examination, and now systematically enforces it on all Candidates. The previous Medical Examination (viz., in Physics, Chemistry, Botany, Materia Medica, and Descriptive Anatomy), is now compulsory.

The Queen's University in Ireland has instituted Clinical Examinations in Medicine and Surgery in the final Examinations for the M.D. and Master in Surgery.

The Royal College of Surgeons of Ireland had formerly instituted a Practical Examination in Bandaging, &c., and its Council has now ordered Clinical Examinations in Surgery and in Medicine for the final Examination.

The King and Queen's College of Physicians has instituted a Clinical Examination, which is carried on in the Wards of an Hospital for the second or final part of the Examination.

The Apothecaries' Hall of Ireland has extended the period of Examination from two to six days, so as to test more practically the Candidate's knowledge, and they have instituted a Clinical Examination of Patients which is enforced on all Candidates.

It cannot be doubted, from the previous statements, which have been drawn from official communications received from each Licensing Body, that great progress has been made in the path indicated in the various Reports of the Visitors of the Medical Council, and of the Committee on Education.

There are, however, some suggestions in the Education Report which have not yet been carried out, and on which it seems desirable the Council should express an opinion, while there are other suggestions which it will be better to keep in abeyance.

Of the former kind, there are some of considerable importance :—

1st. The separation of the teaching of Pharmacy and Therapeutics, the former being made an early, and the latter a late course in the Curriculum. It seems desirable that the instruction in Pharmacy should be separated from that in Therapeutics, and that the former should be obtained at an early, and the latter at a later period of the Professional Curriculum. So, also, it will be for consideration how far practical instruction in drugs and pharmaceutical preparations might not be substituted for formal Lectures. In the last two Sessions a plan of this kind has been carried on in Aberdeen.

2nd. The recommendation that Pathological Anatomy should be made a separate course has not been carried out in all cases, but several of the Licensing Bodies have endeavoured to meet it by requiring a certificate of attendance, and of practical instruction in the Dead House.

It is desirable that systematic instruction in Pathological Anatomy should form a part of Professional Education.

3rd. The Committee on Education strongly advised the enforcement of more regular Class Examinations. Certain of the Licensing Bodies have ordered that all Students shall produce evidence of having undergone these Examinations, and it is desirable that all the Licensing Bodies should issue Regulations that Class Examinations shall form a necessary part of every course of instruction.

The other points raised in the Education Report of 1869, and which we advise should not be discussed at present, are—the length of the Sessions, the method of teaching Chemistry, and the application of Chemistry to Physiology and Pathology, the teaching of Minute Anatomy, and the definition of the areas of Instruction and of Examination

The Council will doubtless remember that the Education Report of 1869 strongly recommended the formation of Conjoint Examining Boards, so as to reduce the number of Examinations for Licences to practise, and to make each Licence a Qualification in both Medicine and Surgery ; that the Council authorized circulars to the Licensing Bodies in this sense, and that in the autumn of 1869 various conferences took place between some of the Licensing Bodies, and replies were received from many of them favourable to the proposed combinations. Subsequently the action of the Government in introducing a Bill suspended all negotiations of the kind.

The withdrawal of that Bill makes it desirable that these negotiations be resumed.

It might indeed be argued that the willingness of the Licensing Bodies to improve their Examinations, and the fact that they really have improved them, renders it less necessary to revive the plan of an uniform Examination for each division of the Kingdom. But a moment's reflection will show that the proposal is still necessary.

The independent Examinations for Licences being as numerous as ever, the risk of inequality of standard in different parts of the Kingdom still obtains.

This inequality may doubtless be to a certain degree corrected by more constant and systematic visitations, but the only effectual remedy in the opinion of the Council is the consolidation of Examinations.

In a Resolution, which was carried by 17 votes against 1 on the 26th of February, 1870, the Council decided that it was of opinion that a Joint Examining Board should be formed in each division of the Kingdom. It is, therefore, desirable that the Council should address a letter to each Licensing Body, transmitting a copy of the Resolution of the 26th February, 1870, and urging that arrangements for the formation of the Boards shall be undertaken without delay.

(Signed)   E. A. PARKES,
Chairman.

Moved by Dr. PARKES; *Seconded* by Dr. ANDREW WOOD; and *Agreed to :*

"That the Report of the Committee on Professional Education as now Amended be received and adopted, and that copies be sent to the several Licensing Bodies for their consideration."

2. *Moved* by Dr. PARKES and *Seconded* by Dr. ANDREW WOOD :

"That in case the arrangements for Conjoint Examining Boards are not completed in each Division of the Kingdom by the close of the year, in accordance with the recommendations of the Council on the subject, the Executive Committee shall be authorized to seek an interview with the Lord President of the Privy Council and to urge upon him the desirability of such Medical Legislation in the Session of 1872 as may carry out the object the General Medical Council had in view, in passing the Resolutions of the 26th and 28th February, 1870, and of the 7th July, 1871."

3. Amendment *Moved* by Dr. ALEXANDER WOOD, and *Seconded* by Dr. STORRAR:

"That a Meeting of the General Medical Council be held early in 1872, to receive the proposals of the Bodies for Conjoint Examinations, and to consider whether any, and what steps should be taken to carry out the Resolutions of the Council in favour of such combinations."

The Amendment was *Carried*, and having been put as a Substantive Motion was again *Carried*.

4. *Read*—The following Report of the Committee on the Registration of Medical Students, and the Returns from the Bodies in Schedule (A) of Professional Examinations and their Results:

REPORT.

1. The following Table has been compiled from the Returns according to Recommendation 6, sec. v. (Professional Examination), of the Recommendations of the Council, 1866 (*see* Vol. iv., p. 311), viz., "that Returns from the Licensing Bodies be made annually on the 1st of January, to the General Medical Council, stating the number and names of the Candidates who have passed their first as well as their second Examinations, and the number of those who have been rejected at the first and second Examinations respectively."

This Table has been submitted in form of proof to the Registrars of the Licensing Bodies for revision, and the Committee have every reason to believe it correct.

TABLE FOR 1870.

Licensing Bodies.	Qualifications.	No. of Exams.	No. Passed. 1st Exam.	No. Passed. 2nd Exam.	No. Passed. Final.	No. Rejected. 1st Exam.	No. Rejected. 2nd Exam.	No. Rejected. Final.
R. Coll. Phys. London	Membership	3	3	...	17	...	...	4
	Licence	2	...	...	51	2	...	13
	Fellowship	2	62	...	26	22	...	6
R. Coll. Surg. England	Membership	2	404	...	307	187	...	64
	Licence in Midwify	1	...	...	8	...	...	3
Soc. Apothecaries, London	Licence	2	189	...	204	50	...	46
University of Oxford	M.B.	2	3	...	2	2	...	...
	M.D.	Essay	...	...	...	...	...	...
	M.B.	3	16	6	11	3	4	5
University of Cambridge	M.D.	Essay	...	...	...	...	...	...
	M.C.	1*	...	...	...	...	...	1
	M.B.	1	...	...	1	...	...	...
University of Durham	M.D.	Essay	...	...	...	...	...	...
	L.M.	2	...	...	...	...	...	...
	M.C.	2	...	...	...	...	...	...
			1st M.B.		2nd M.B.			
University of London	M.B.	2	34†	...	24	22	...	...
R. Coll. Phys. Edinburgh	Licence	2	9	...	107	6	...	30
R. Coll. Surg. Edinburgh	Licence	2	1	...	41	3	...	9
R. Coll. Phys. and R. Coll. Surg. Edinburgh	Licence in Med. and Surg.	2	41	...	80	34	...	34
R. Coll. Phys. Edin. & Fac. Phys. Surg. Glasg.	Licence in Med. and Surg.	2	6	...	19	1	...	10
Fac. Phys. Surg. Glasg.	Licence	2	38	...	24	28	...	26
	M.D.	...	...	...	...	...	...	...
University of Aberdeen	M.B. and M.C.	3	55	36	32‡	9	5	6
	M.B.	...	...	...	...	...	...	...
	M.D.	...	...	...	...	...	...	...
University of Edinburgh	M.B. and M.C.	3	87	84	58§	42	33	15
	M.B.	...	...	...	...	...	...	...
	M.B.	3	34	39	43	15	11	11
University of Glasgow	M.D.	...	1	...	3	...	...	...
	M.C.	...	...	...	...	...	...	...
University of St. Andrew's	M.D.	1	...	...	10	...	...	...
K. & Q. Coll. Phys. Ireland	Licence in Medicine	2	...	...	97	2	...	11
	Ditto in Midwifery	1	...	...	78	...	...	17
	Licence	...	118	96	96	36	12	16
R. Coll. Surg. Ireland	Fellowship	3	8	8	8	1	1	1
	Licence in Midwify	...	...	...	13	...	...	1
Apothecaries' Hall, Ireland	Licence	2	20	...	19	2	2	...
			1st M.B.		Deg. M.B.	1st M.B.		Deg. M.B.
University of Dublin	M.B.	3	10	...	31	63¶	...	2
	M.C.	...	...	...	17	...	...	4
	M.D.	2	81	...	42	54	...	8
Queen's University Ireland	M.C.	1	...	...	32	...	...	...
	M.D. and M.C.	...	...	...	...	...	...	...

* Preceded by the 3 M.B. Examinations.
† Of this number, 2 were examined in Physiology only, and 2 passed without Physiology.
‡ Of these, 30 took M.B. and C.M., and 2 M.B. alone.
§ Of these, 50 took M.B. and C.M., 4 M.B. alone, and 4 M.D. In addition 28 M.B.'s gave in their Theses for M.D., which were approved by the Medical Faculty, and they were accordingly promoted to that Degree.
¶ Not passed in all subjects.

2. The subjoined is a statement of the numbers of Students registered in the following years. The numbers are:

	1866.	1867.	1868.	1869.	1870.
In ENGLAND.	477	457	483	530	551
In SCOTLAND	302	258	266	317	341
In IRELAND .	157	212	175	317	268
Total . .	936	927	924	1,164	1,160

(Signed)   D. EMBLETON,
Chairman.

The foregoing Report was referred to the Executive Committee.

The hour of Six having arrived, on the Motion of the President the Standing Orders were suspended.

5. *Read*—The following Report of the Committee on the Visitation of Examinations:

REPORT.

The Committee on this subject appointed on the 8th inst. beg to report—

1. That in their opinion the time has now come when an interchange of Visitors between the three Branch Councils would strengthen confidence in the Visitation, and would tend to assimilate the character of the Examinations of the various Boards.

2. That with the view of carrying out the Resolution of the Council of 8th July, a Committee of Visitors be appointed to make arrangements what Examinations should be visited, and for carrying out the Visitation.

3. That the Committee of Visitors consist of eight, four to be elected by the English Branch Council, and two by the Scottish and Irish Branch Councils respectively.

4. That each Examination reported on shall be visited by a due proportion of Members of the Branch Councils, other than the one in that division of the Kingdom where the Examination is conducted.

5. That it is not desirable that Visitations should take place in the case of those Examining Boards with regard to which it shall appear to the Visitation Committee that there is a reasonable prospect of a Conjoint Examination being formed.

(Signed) ALEXANDER WOOD,
Chairman.

July 10*th*, 1871.

The Consideration of the foregoing Report was referred to the next Meeting of the Medical Council.

6. *Moved* by Dr. A. SMITH; *Seconded* by Dr. STORRAR; and *Agreed to :*

"That the powers and duties heretofore delegated to the Executive Committee shall be vested in the Committee until the next Meeting of the General Medical Council."

7. *Moved* by Dr. A. SMITH; *Seconded* by Dr. STORRAR; and *Agreed to :*

"That the sum of Five Guineas be given to the Hall Porter at 32, Soho Square."

8. *Moved* by Dr. A. SMITH; *Seconded* by Dr. STORRAR; and *Agreed to*:

> "That the cordial thanks of this Council are due, and are hereby tendered, to Dr. ANDREW WOOD, for his services as Chairman of the Business Committee, during the present Session of the Council."

9. *Moved* by Dr. A. SMITH; *Seconded* by Dr. STORRAR; and *Agreed to*:

> "That the thanks of the Council are hereby cordially tendered to Dr. PAGET, the President, for his efficient services during the present Session of the Medical Council."

Confirmed—GEORGE EDWARD PAGET, M.D.,
President.

July 10*th*, 1871.

(No. 146.)

GENERAL COUNCIL

OF

MEDICAL EDUCATION & REGISTRATION.

MINUTES OF ADJOURNED MEETING, MONDAY, JULY 10, 1871.

32, Soho Square, London, W.

Present—

Dr. PAGET, *President*, in the Chair.

Dr. HUMPHRY.	Dr. MACROBIN.
Dr. EMBLETON.	Dr. THOMSON.
Dr. STORRAR.	Dr. PARKES.
Dr. ANDREW WOOD.	Dr. QUAIN.
Dr. FLEMING.	

Dr. FRANCIS HAWKINS, *Registrar.*

The Minutes of the preceding Meeting were read and confirmed.

(*No.* 100.)

EXECUTIVE COMMITTEE

OF THE

GENERAL COUNCIL

OF

MEDICAL EDUCATION & REGISTRATION.

32, Soho Square, London, W.
January 25th, 1871.

Present—

Dr. PAGET, *President*, in the Chair.

Dr. BENNETT.   Dr. A. SMITH.

Dr. ACLAND.   Dr. SHARPEY.

Dr. FRANCIS HAWKINS, *Registrar*.

The Minutes of the last Meeting were read and confirmed.

1. The vacancy in the Executive Committee, caused by Mr. CÆSAR HAWKINS having ceased to be a Member of the Medical Council, was filled up by the Election of Dr. QUAIN.

2. The Annual Accounts and Balance Sheets of the General and Branch Councils were examined and considered, and the further consideration of them was adjourned to the next meeting of the Committee: it was *Resolved* that they should be submitted to a professional Accountant, whose opinion should be taken as to the general arrangement of the Accounts.

3. *Ordered*—That the *Medical Register* for 1871 be published; and that 750 copies be printed, in addition to the 2,000 copies to be furnished for distribution by the Government; but that 500 copies only be, for the present, bound.

REPORT.

The Treasurers report that, in pursuance of the Resolution of the General Council of February 24th, 1870 (Minutes, vol. viii., p. 17), they have consulted with Mr. GREG, the Comptroller of H.M. Stationery Office, on the practicability of reducing the expense of publishing the *Medical Register*, and have learned from him that the present charge is at a considerably higher rate than is paid for work of equal quality executed for the Stationery Office.

They further report that Mr. GREG was ready to assist the Council in the matter, either by negotiating a fresh contract on more favourable terms with the present or some other printer, or by undertaking to have the work executed, "on a pay account," through the Stationery Office, charging 5 per cent. to the Council on the whole expense. Mr. GREG also pointed out that the *breadth* of the page might be somewhat contracted without detracting from the appearance of the book or the facility of reference.

The expense for 3,000 copies, binding included, if printed by the Stationery Office, was estimated

at £426 8s. for the first year,

and £336 8s. for the next and succeeding years.

In case of terminating the existing contract with Mr. KELLY, a year's rent of the type would have to be paid.

The amount paid by the Council last year for 3,000 copies, including £91 for rent of type, was £609 14s. 6d.

(Signed)   W. SHARPEY.
RICHARD QUAIN.

January 25th, 1871.

Resolved—That, seeing the very considerable saving that may be effected, were the printing and binding of the *Medical Register* executed by the Stationery Office, that course be adopted, commencing with the publication for 1872; and that notice be forthwith given to Mr. KELLY that the type will not be required after printing the requisite impression for 1871.

4. *Ordered*—That an Alphabetical List be prepared and printed of all the Students registered during the year 1870. That the number of copies printed be 250. That two copies be supplied to each of the Bodies enumerated in Schedule (A) to the Medical Act, and one copy to each of the Medical Schools and Hospitals.

5. *Ordered*—That the Eighth Volume of the Minutes of the Medical Council and Executive Committee be printed for the year 1870.

Confirmed—GEORGE EDWARD PAGET, M.D.,
President.

February 24th, 1871.

(*No.* 101.)

EXECUTIVE COMMITTEE

OF THE

GENERAL COUNCIL

OF

MEDICAL EDUCATION & REGISTRATION.

32, Soho Square, London, W.

February 24*th*, 1871.

Present—

Dr. Paget, *President*, in the Chair.

Dr. Bennett.	Dr. Sharpey.
Dr. Acland.	Dr. Quain.
Dr. A. Smith.	

Dr. Francis Hawkins, *Registrar.*

The Minutes of the last Meeting were read and confirmed.

1. The adjourned consideration of the Annual Accounts and Balance Sheets of the General and Branch Councils was resumed.

Read—A Letter from Messrs. QUILTER, BALL & Co., the Professional Accountants consulted in accordance with the Resolution passed by the Executive Committee at its last meeting.—(*See* Minutes, vol. ix. Ex. Com., p. 2, s. 2.)

The Accountants stated in their letter that the general arrangement of the Accounts of the Council appeared to them to be satisfactory.

The Accounts and Balance Sheets having been approved, it was *Ordered*—That they should be circulated with the Minutes. And that, pursuant to Sect. 44 of the Medical Act (1858), Returns of the Accounts of the General and Branch Councils be laid before both Houses of Parliament in the month of March, and published with the Minutes and with the *Medical Register*.

2. *Resolved*—That, in order to carry into effect the Resolution, passed by the Executive Committee at their last Meeting, respecting the publication of the *Medical Register*, the Treasurers be requested to make the necessary arrangements with the Comptroller of H.M. Stationery Office, for the printing and binding of the *Medical Register*.

The REGISTRAR informed the Committee that he had given notice to Mr. KELLY that the type of the *Medical Register* will not be required after printing the requisite impression of 1871.

Read—A letter from Mr. KELLY, with reference to the notice above-mentioned. The REGISTRAR was directed to inform Mr. KELLY that his letter had been received and read to the Committee.

3. In discharge of the annual duty delegated to it by the General Council, the Committee proceeded to revise the Recognized List of Examining Bodies, whose Examinations fulfil the conditions of the Medical Council as regards the Preliminary Education.

Read—A Letter from the VICE-CHANCELLOR of the University of Melbourne, in which it was stated that the Council of that University, ever desirous of maintaining a high standard of Education, and anxious to adopt any Regulations recommended by the Medical Council for the advancement of Medical Science, had passed a Series of Regulations, " On Preliminary Examination for Students in Medicine," which have been framed for the purpose of making the Examinations of the University of Melbourne fulfil the conditions of the Medical Council. These regulations were to come into force at the commencement of the present year.

Confirmed—GEORGE EDWARD PAGET, M.D.,
President.

July 3rd, 1871.

BALA[N

1871.—J
To R[e
Balances
Cash

Cash

At [
In [

Ded

Registra[
447
33
228

BALANCE "CASH ACCOUNT" of the BRANCH COUNCIL for ENGLAND of the GENERAL COUNCIL of MEDICAL EDUCATION and REGISTRATION of the UNITED KINGDOM, for the Year ending January 5th, 1871.

1871.—Jan. 5.		£ s. d.	£ s. d.
To RECEIPTS:			
Balances as per last Statement, viz.:			
Cash paid by Branch Council for Scotland (1869)		611 1 9	
Cash paid by Branch Council for Ireland (1869)		713 5 8	
At Bankers		143 0 5	
In Registrar's hands		20 14 6½	
		1488 2 4½	
Deduct Loan repaid to Pharmacopœia Account, as per last Statement		286 5 0	
			1201 17 4½
Registration Fees, viz.:			
447 at £5 0 0 each		2235 0 0	
33 at 2 0 0 „		66 0 0	
229 at 0 5 0 „		57 0 0	
		2358 0 0	
One Year's Dividend on £23,000 Three per Cent. Consols		677 1 3	
Total Receipts, Branch Council for England (1870)			3036 1 3
			£4236 18 7½

1871.—Jan. 5.								
By DISBURSEMENTS:								
Fees to Members of Branch Council, viz.:								

Names.	No. of Sittings.	Fees.			Travelling Expenses.		Total.	
		£	s.	d.	£ s. d.		£ s. d.	
The President	1	2	2	0	2 2 0		4 4 0	
Dr. Bennett	1	2	2	0	...		2 2 0	
Mr. Quain	1	2	2	0	...		2 2 0	
Mr. Cooper	1	2	2	0	...		2 2 0	
Dr. Humphry	1	2	2	0	2 2 0		4 4 0	
Dr. Embleton	1	2	2	0	6 6 0		8 8 0	
Dr. Storrar	1	2	2	0	...		2 2 0	
Dr. Quain	1	2	2	0	...		2 2 0	
Dr. Rumsey	1	2	2	0	4 4 0		6 6 0	
		18 18 0			14 14 0		33 12 0	

		£ s. d.	£ s. d.
Fees		18 18 0	
Travelling Expenses		14 14 0	
			33 12 0
Salaries:			
Registrar, one year, to November 25th		200 0 0	
Clerks, one year, to December 25th		200 0 0	
			400 0 0
Stationery			3 19 6
Printing			5 3 6
Postage			25 1 8
Rent			60 0 0
Gratuity to Hall Porter			8 8 0
Office Furniture			29 14 6
Sundries (including Messenger)			12 19 7
Expenses of Branch Council for England (1870)			597 18 9
Per-Centage Rate, English Branch Council, paid to General Council			1948 7 4
Total Amount paid by Branch Council for England (1870)			2546 6 1
Cash lent to Branch Council for Scotland (1870), being the per-centage rate		£509 15 8	
„ „ „ Ireland (1870)		714 13 9	
At Bankers		448 3 5	
In Registrar's hands		17 19 8½	
			1690 12 6½
			£4236 18 7½

Examined, compared with the Vouchers, and found correct.

(Signed) JAS. R. BENNETT, M.D.

JOHN STORRAR, M.D.

January 24th, 1871.

STATEMENT OF THE RECEIPTS AND EXPENDITURE OF THE GENERAL COUNCIL, AND PER-CENTAGE RATE Chargeable to the Three Branch Councils for England, Scotland, and Ireland, of the said General Council of Medical Education and Registration of the United Kingdom.

1871.—January 6.
To Receipts:

	£ s. d.	£ s. d.	£ s. d.
To Cash for Sale of Registers, viz.:			
2000 copies supplied to Government	250 0 0		
108 to Booksellers at 3s. 6d. per copy	18 18 0		
7 Trade allowance.			
6 at 4s. per copy	1 12 0		
		270 10 0	
370 Copies supplied without charge to those persons who registered in 1862, who applied for them, viz.:—			
2400 { 143 England.			
100 Scotland.			
130 Ireland.			
To Cash for Penalty—re Robert Wilson		0 10 0	
To Cash for Sale of Pharmacopœia (1870)		270 0 0	
To Balance transferred to General Council (Minutes, Vol. viii, p. 61.)		337 0 0	
			887 15 0
To Cash advanced by Branch Council for England, on account of General Council (being 64½ per Cent. on £4642 6s. 10d., the total receipts of the several Branch Councils, plus 0s. 10d.—*see below*)			3172 10 6

PER-CENTAGE CALCULATION.

Receipts of the Branch Councils respectively:

	Fees.	Interest.	Total.
	£ s. d.	£ s. d.	£ s. d.
England	2358 0 0	677 1 3	3035 1 3
Scotland	725 10 0	68 11 2	794 1 2
Ireland	1047 5 0	66 10 3	1113 4 5
	£4130 15 0	£811 11 10	£4942 6 10

Per-Centage payable by each of the Three Branch Councils:

	£ s. d.	£ s. d.	s. d.
England } At	on 3035 1 3 will pay 1618 2 4 deficiency 6 0		
Scotland } 64½ per cent.	on 794 1 2 will pay 600 13 8 deficiency 2 0		
Ireland }	on 1113 4 5 will pay 714 10 11 deficiency 2 10		

Total Receipts	£4942 6 10
Total Per-Centage Rate payable to the General Council	£3172 16 0

£4060 11 9

1871.—January 6.
By Disbursements:
Fees to Members of Council to January 5, 1871, viz.:

Names.	Fees for Attendance at General Council	Additional Fees beyond 200 miles	Travelling Expenses, General Council	Hotel Expenses	Fees for Attendance at Ex. Com. and additional Fees beyond 200 miles	Travelling and Hotel Expenses, Executive Com.	Totals.
	£ s.	£ s.	£ s.	£ s.	£ s.	£ s.	£ s.
The President	57 15	..	4 4	13 13	18 18	18 18	110 8
Bennett, Dr.	57 15	..	..	..	18 18	..	76 13
Hawkins, Mr.	57 15	..	..	..	18 18	..	76 13
Cooper, Mr.	57 15	..	..	..	..	..	57 15
Acland, Dr.	57 15	..	4 4	13 13	12 12	12 12	100 16
Humphry, Dr.	57 15	..	4 4	13 13	..	..	75 12
Embleton, Dr.	57 15	10 10	12 12	13 13	..	..	94 10
Storrar, Dr.	57 15	..	..	..	..	..	57 16
Wood, Dr. Alex.	57 15	21 0	18 18	13 13	..	..	111 6
Wood, Dr. Andrew.	57 15	21 0	18 18	13 13	14 14	22 1	148 1
Fleming, Dr.	57 15	21 0	18 18	13 13	..	..	111 6
Macrobin, Dr.	57 15	21 0	18 18	13 13	..	..	111 6
Thomson, Dr.	57 15	21 0	18 18	13 13	..	..	111 6
Smith, Dr.	57 15	21 0	18 18	13 13	29 8	39 18	178 10
Hargrave, Mr.	57 15	21 0	19 16	13 13	..	..	105 4
Leet, Dr.	57 15	21 0	18 18	13 13	..	..	102 4
Apjohn, Dr.	57 15	21 0	18 18	13 13	..	..	109 4
Corrigan, Sir D., Bt.	57 15	21 0	18 18	13 13	..	..	109 4
Sharpey, Dr.	57 15	..	..	..	18 18	..	76 13
Parkes, Dr.	57 15	..	4 4	13 13	..	..	75 12
Quain, Dr.	52 10	..	..	..	..	..	52 10
Rumsey, Dr.	26 5	..	4 4	0 0	..	..	30 15
Stokes, Dr.	47 5	21 0	10 10	11 11	..	..	96 12
Christison, Dr.	31 10	10 10	0 6	7 7	..	..	59 10
	1312 10	252 0	236 7	226 10	132 6	93 0	2258 11

	£ s. d.	£ s. d.
Fees to Members for Attendance at General Council	1312 10 0	
Additional Fees beyond 200 miles	252 0 0	
Travelling Expenses on account of General Council	236 7 0	
Hotel Expenses	226 10 0	
		2032 10 0
Fees for Attendance at Executive Committees	107 2 0	
Additional Fees beyond 200 miles	25 4 0	
Travelling Expenses	94 0 0	
Hotel Expenses	0 0 0	
		226 13 0
		£2258 11 0
Salaries:		
Registrar, to 25th November, 1870	500 0 0	
Clerks, to 25th December, 1870	250 0 0	
		540 0 0
Printing:		
Register, 3000 Copies	560 7 0	
Binding 500	18 15 0	
Quarterly Lists of New Names	30 12 0	
Register of Students	21 4 0	
Minutes, Programmes, &c., at Meeting of General Council in 1870 (2 Sessions)	181 17 0	
Medical Education Reports	66 15 8	
State Medicine Reports	3 10 0	
Executive Committee	23 0 0	
Eighth volume of Minutes (first portion)	32 18 0	
General Printing	24 6 4	
		875 5 4
Rent		40 0 0
Law Expenses (incurred in 1869)		49 15 0
Postage		22 10 5
Stationery		20 19 0
Advertisements		39 3 0
Penalties contributed to defray expenses of Prosecutions		0 19 0
Incidentals:		
Expenses (including Refreshments) at the General Council Meeting in 1870 (First Session)	15 2 0	
Ditto (Second Session)	21 16 11	
Gratuity to the Officials at the College of Physicians, College of Surgeons, and Soho Square (the Porter)	33 12 0	
Assistance in making up the list of 2000 names for the Stationery Office, for circulating the Register	3 10 0	
Sundries (including Messenger)	34 4 7	
		108 5 6
		£4060 11 0

RETURNS ENERAL COUNCIL, and of the
B ng January 5th, 1871, pursuant to
Se

NDITURE.
L COUNCIL.

1871.		£	s.	d.	£	s.	d.
Jan. 5.	To Council for						
	„ l Meetings	1312	10	0			
	„ bers of Coun-						
	„ 00 miles from						
	. . .	252	0	0			
	„ account of						
	. . .	238	7	0			
	„ (. . .	229	19	0			
					2032	16	0
	uncil for At-						
	Committees,						
	ond 200 miles	132	6	0			
„ Divid	xpenses	93	9	0			
	Clerks				550	0	0
„ Divi	Quarterly						
	C . . .	609	14	6			
	nts . .	24	4	0			
„ Cash	nd Educa-						
„ Cash	. .	73	3	6			
„ Cash	ge, Adver-						
	bursements	492	4	9			
	s defraying						
	h . .	9	19	0			
					1209	5	9
	1869) . .				42	15	0
	OF GENERAL MEDICAL						
	. . . .				4060	11	9
	ENGLISH						
	. . .	564	6	9			
	avelling .	33	12	0			
					597	18	9
	SCOTCH						
	. . .	221	15	3			
	avelling .	18	18	0			
					240	13	3
	H BRANCH						
	. .	254	4	10			
	. .	33	12	0			
					287	16	10
	H BRANCH						
	. .	1690	12	6½			
	H BRANCH						
	. .	471	13	6			
		2162	6	0½			
	CH COUNCIL	273	3	6			
					1889	2	6½
					£7076	3	1½

AM SHARPEY, M.D., } *Treasurers.*
RD QUAIN, M.D.,   }
IS HAWKINS, M.D., *Registrar.*

RETURNS to both HOUSES of PARLIAMENT of RECEIPTS and EXPENDITURE of the GENERAL COUNCIL, and of the BRANCH COUNCILS for England, Scotland, and Ireland respectively, for the Year ending January 5th, 1871, pursuant to Section XLIV. of the Medical Act (1858).

RECEIPTS.
GENERAL COUNCIL.

1871.		£ s. d.	£ s. d.
Jan. 5.	To Cash for sale of Registers	270 16 0	
	„ Cash for sale of Pharmacopœia	607 6 0	
	„ Cash for Penalty	9 10 0	
	„ Cash from Branch Council for England, its proportion of Disbursements	1918 7 4	
	„ Cash from Branch Council for Scotland, its proportion of Disbursements	609 14 8	
	„ Cash from Branch Council for Ireland, its proportion of Disbursements	714 18 9	3172 16 9
			£4059 11 9

EXPENDITURE.
GENERAL COUNCIL.

1871.		£ s. d.	£ s. d.
Jan. 5.	By Fees to Members of Council for Attendance at General Meetings	1312 10 0	
	„ Fees (additional) to Members of Council who reside beyond 200 miles from London	262 0 0	
	„ Travelling Expenses on account of General Council	238 7 0	
	„ Hotel Expenses	229 19 0	2042 16 0
	„ Fees to Members of Council for Attendance at Executive Committees, and additional fees beyond 200 miles	132 6 0	
	„ Travelling and Hotel Expenses	23 8 0	
	„ Salaries (Registrar and Clerks)		225 18 0
	„ Printing Registers and Quarterly Lists		500 0 0
	„ Printing Register of Students		600 11 0
	„ Printing State Medicine and Educational Reports		24 4 0
			73 3 6
	„ Law Expenses (incurred in 1960)		42 15 0
	„ Penalty contributed towards defraying Expenses of Prosecution		9 10 0
	„ Printing, Stationery, Postage, Advertising, Rent, and other Disbursements		192 4 0
			£4059 11 9

ENGLISH BRANCH COUNCIL.

1871.		£ s. d.	£ s. d.
Jan. 5.	To Balance on 5th January, 1870		1208 17 4½
	„ Cash for 23 Fees, at £3 each	69 0 0	
	„ Cash for 447 Fees, at £5 each	2235 0 0	
	„ Cash for 228 Fees, at 5s. each	57 0 0	2358 0 0
	„ Dividends on £73,000 Three per Cent. Consols		677 1 3
			£4236 15 7½

1871.		£ s. d.	£ s. d.
Jan. 5.	By Fees to Council for Attendance and Travelling Expenses		33 12 0
	„ Salaries, Stationery, Printing, Postage, and other Disbursements		564 6 9
	„ Per-Centage Rate, pursuant to Sect. XIII. of the Medical Act		1948 7 1
	„ Balance		1690 13 9½
			£4236 15 7½

SCOTTISH BRANCH COUNCIL.

1871.		£ s. d.	£ s. d.
Jan. 5.	To Balance in Bank on 5th January, 1870		429 1 2
	„ Cash for 140 Fees, at £5 each	700 0 0	
	„ Cash for 5 Fees at £2 each	10 0 0	
	„ Cash for 67 Fees, at 5s. each	16 15 0	726 10 0
	„ Dividends on £2000 Three per Cent. Consols		66 17 0
	„ Interest allowed by Bank of Scotland on account of 1869		9 4 8
	„ Sale of Registers		0 9 0
			£1232 2 4

1871.		£ s. d.	£ s. d.
Jan. 5.	By Fees to Council for Attendance and Travelling Expenses		19 16 0
	„ Salaries, Printing, Stationery, Advertisements, Rent, and other Disbursements		221 18 8
	„ Per-Centage Rate, pursuant to Sect. XIII. of the Medical Act		609 16 8
	„ Balance		471 13 0
			£1232 2 4

IRISH BRANCH COUNCIL.

1871.		£ s. d.	£ s. d.
Jan. 5.	To Cash for 2 Fees, at £2 each	4 0 0	
	„ Cash for 205 Fees, at £5 each	1025 0 0	
	„ Cash for 72 Fees, at 5s. each	18 0 0	1047 0 0
	„ Dividend on £2261 3s. 2d. New Three per Cent. Consols		66 19 5
	„ Balance		213 3 6
			£1326 7 11

1871.		£ s. d.	£ s. d.
Jan. 5.	By Balance due on 5th January, 1870		349 17 3
	„ Fees to Council		33 12 0
	„ Salaries, Printing, Stationery, Advertising, Rent, and other Disbursements		234 4 10
	„ Per-Centage Rate, pursuant to Sect. XIII. of the Medical Act		711 13 2
			£1326 7 11

GENERAL SUMMARY.

RECEIPTS.

1871.		£ s. d.	£ s. d.	£ s. d.
Jan. 5.	To Balance in hand, Branch Council for England, January 5th, 1870	1208 17 4½		
	„ Balance in hand, Branch Council for Scotland, January 5th, 1870	429 1 2		
		1638 18 7½		
	Deduct, Branch Council for Ireland	349 17 3	1288 1 4½	
	„ Cash for 162 Fees at £3 each	2040 0 0		
	„ Cash for 40 Fees at £2 each	80 0 0		
	„ Cash for 362 Fees at 5s. each	90 15 0	4130 15 0	
	„ Dividends on Stock, English Branch Council	677 1 3		
	„ Dividends on Stock, Scottish Branch Council	66 17 0		
	„ Dividends on Stock, Irish Branch Council	66 19 5	811 8 10	
	„ Cash for sale of Pharmacopœia in 1870		607 6 0	
	„ Cash for sale of Registers in 1870		270 19 0	
	„ Cash for Penalties		9 10 0	
				£7076 3 1½

EXPENDITURE.

1871.		£ s. d.	£ s. d.	£ s. d.
Jan. 5.	By Fees to Members for Attendance at General Council	1312 10 0		
	„ Additional Fees to Members residing beyond 200 miles from London	262 0 0		
	„ Travelling Expenses	238 7 0		
	„ Hotel Expenses to non-resident Members of General Council	229 19 0	2042 16 0	
	„ Fees and Additional Fees for Attendance at Executive Committee	132 6 0		
	„ Travelling and Hotel Expenses to non-resident Members of the Executive Committee	23 8 0		
	„ Salaries to Registrar and Clerks	225 15 0		
	„ Printing the Register and Quarterly Lists	500 0 0		
	„ Printing Register of Students	600 11 0		
	„ Printing State Medicine and Educational Reports	24 4 0		
	„ Printing, Stationery, Postage, Advertising, Rent, & other Disbursements	73 3 6		
	„ Penalty contributed towards defraying Expenses of Prosecution	192 1 9		
			9 10 0	1509 5 0
	„ Law Expenses (incurred in 1869)			13 14 0
	TOTAL EXPENDITURE OF GENERAL MEDICAL COUNCIL IN 1870			1040 11 9
	„ Salaries, Printing, &c., ENGLISH BRANCH COUNCIL	561 8 9		
	„ Fees for Attendance and Travelling	33 12 0	597 16 9	
	„ Salaries, Printing, &c., SCOTCH BRANCH COUNCIL	221 15 8		
	„ Fees for Attendance and Travelling	19 16 0	240 15 3	
	„ Salaries, Printing, &c., IRISH BRANCH COUNCIL	751 4 10		
	„ Fees for Attendance	33 12 0	297 16 10	
	„ Balance to credit of ENGLISH BRANCH COUNCIL		1690 13 6½	
	„ Balance to credit of SCOTCH BRANCH COUNCIL		471 13 0	
			2162 6 6½	
	Deduct Balance, IRISH BRANCH COUNCIL		213 3 5	1949 3 1½
				£7076 3 1½

(Signed) WILLIAM SHARPEY, M.D., } Treasurers.
RICHARD QUAIN, M.D.,
FRANCIS HAWKINS, M.D., Registrar.

(*No.* 102.)

EXECUTIVE COMMITTEE

OF THE

GENERAL COUNCIL

OF

MEDICAL EDUCATION & REGISTRATION.

32, SOHO SQUARE, LONDON, W.

July 3rd, 1871.

Present—

Dr. PAGET, *President*, in the Chair.

Dr. BENNETT.   Dr. A. SMITH.
Dr. ACLAND.   Dr. QUAIN.
Dr. ANDREW WOOD.

Dr. FRANCIS HAWKINS, *Registrar*.

The Minutes of the last Meeting were read and confirmed.

In accordance with the Standing Order, Cap. VII., Sect. 16, the Committee prepared and arranged the business for the consideration of the General Council.

(No. 39.)

BRANCH COUNCIL FOR ENGLAND

OF THE

GENERAL COUNCIL

OF

MEDICAL EDUCATION & REGISTRATION.

32, Soho Square, London, W.
April 27th, 1871.

Present—

Dr. PAGET, *President*, in the Chair.

Dr. BENNETT.	Dr. HUMPHRY.
Mr. QUAIN.	Dr. EMBLETON.
Mr. COOPER.	Dr. STORRAR.
Dr. ACLAND.	Dr. QUAIN.

Dr. FRANCIS HAWKINS, *Registrar*.

The Minutes of the last Meeting were read and confirmed.

1. The President communicated to the Branch Council that, by a letter addressed to him, as President, Dr. RUMSEY had resigned his appointment as a Member of the General Medical Council.

2. Mr. OUVRY attended this Meeting, for the purpose of advising the Branch Council as to the course which it was desirable to adopt respecting the two cases of complaint, against certain Registered Practitioners, which had been referred to him at the last Meeting.

Resolved—1st., That, after hearing the evidence in the case of Mr. K., as read by Mr. OUVRY, it is, in the opinion of this Branch Council, necessary to bring the whole matter before the General Medical Council; and that Mr. OUVRY be instructed to direct the Registrar as to the due notice to be given to Mr. K., and the proper legal mode of procedure, so that the charge against him of infamous conduct in a professional respect may be finally decided on by the General Medical Council.

2nd., That, after hearing the evidence on the charge adduced by Dr. MASON, the Branch Council on the advice of the Solicitor, resolve to take no public action in the case.

3. The application of a Student to be Registered, accompanied by a Certificate of his having passed the Oxford Local Examinations, Senior, not including Latin, and by a statement of his intention to pass the Cambridge Previous Examination, before proceeding to a Medical Degree, was not acceeded to.

4. An application for Registration was read from Mr. HOGG, late an Assistant-Surgeon in the service of the East India Company, accompanied by documents, the further consideration of which was deferred.

Confirmed—GEORGE EDWARD PAGET, M.D.,
President.

December 12th, 1871.

(*No.* 40.)

BRANCH COUNCIL FOR ENGLAND

OF THE

GENERAL COUNCIL

OF

MEDICAL EDUCATION & REGISTRATION.

32, SOHO SQUARE, LONDON, W.

December 12*th*, 1871.

Present—

Dr. PAGET, *President*, in the Chair.

Dr. BENNETT.	Dr. HUMPHRY.
Mr. QUAIN.	Dr. STORRAR.
Mr. COOPER.	Dr. SHARPEY.
Dr. ACLAND.	Dr. QUAIN.

Dr. FRANCIS HAWKINS, *Registrar*.

The Minutes of the last Meeting were read and confirmed.

I.—Applications for Special Registration.

1. *Ordered*—That the application of Mr. THOMAS HOGG, now resident at Sydney, N.S.W., and formerly in the service of the East India Company, to be placed on the Register, under the 46th Section of the Medical Act, be granted.

2. *Ordered*—That Dr. RICARDO DE REYNA, of Gibraltar, be Registered, under the 46th Section of the Medical Act, as Doctor in Medicine and Surgery of the University of Seville, 1850.

3. *Ordered* — That Dr. JOHN FRANCIS CHURCHILL, now Registered as M.D. St. Andrew's, 1857, be also Registered as M.D. Paris, 1848.

II.—*Resolved*—That Dr. SHARPEY and Dr. STORRAR be appointed Auditors of the Accounts of the Branch Council for the current year.

III.—The Treasurers were directed to contribute, towards defraying the expenses of the Prosecution, £5 15s. 1d., also 10s. for commission, to the Clerk of the Justices at Cranbrook in Kent, out of two Fines, amounting to £10, imposed on JOHN UNDERHILL for infringements of the 40th Section of the Medical Act.

IV.—Permission was granted to each of the Medical Students whose names are contained in the subjoined List, to date his Professional Studies from the time affixed to his name in the

List, evidence having been produced in each case, that Professional Studies had been commenced *bonâ fide* at that time, and that an Examination, recognized by the Medical Council, had been passed by each Student, previously to such commencement of his Professional Studies.

Mr. WM. HENRY WILLIAMS . . . . from July, 1870.
Mr. HENRY ALGERNON HODGSON . . from October, 1868.
Mr. FRANCIS GOODCHILD . from 6th of September, 1871.
Mr. JOSEPH GUEST BOUGHTON . . . . from July, 1869.
Mr. FREDK. CRAPP PEARCE . . from February, 1868.

Confirmed—GEORGE EDWARD PAGET, M.D.,
President.

January 25th, 1872.

(No. 59.)

SCOTTISH BRANCH

OF THE

GENERAL COUNCIL

OF

MEDICAL EDUCATION & REGISTRATION.

PHYSICIANS' HALL, EDINBURGH,
6th January 1871.

Sederunt—

Dr. ALLEN THOMSON, *Chairman.*

Dr. CHRISTISON.   Dr. ALEXANDER WOOD.

Dr. ANDREW WOOD.

Dr. WILLIAM ROBERTSON, *Registrar.*

---

1. The Minutes of last Meeting were read and confirmed.

2. *Read*—Petition from Mr. J. W. H. TRAIL, who had obtained the degree of Master of Arts at Aberdeen University in March 1870, and commenced Medical Study at Aberdeen in May, but who had not been registered as a Medical Student till November 1870.

The Branch Council agreed that Mr. TRAIL'S Medical curriculum shall be held to have commenced on 1st May 1870.

3. The Treasurer's Annual Accounts were read. It was agreed that, after audit, they should be printed and circulated as usual, with the Minutes.

4. The Registrar laid before the Branch Council the whole papers and correspondence relative to the case of Mr. DAVID GIBB, including the statement which, by direction of the Branch Council (see Minutes of 7th January 1870) had been transmitted to Dr. HAWKINS, and the opinion of the Medical Council's Solicitor upon the case.

The Branch Council agreed :—That in accordance with Mr. OUVRY's opinion the papers relative to Mr. GIBB's conduct be now transmitted to the Royal College of Physicians of Edinburgh for their information.

Confirmed—ALLEN THOMSON.

ACCOUNT, Charge and Discharge, of the TREASURERS' Intromissions with the FUNDS of the SCOTTISH BRANCH OF GENERAL MEDICAL COUNCIL, from 5th January 1870 to 5th January 1871.

CHARGE.	£ s. d.	DISCHARGE.	£ s. d.
Balance, Cash in Registrar's hands, on 5th January 1870,	4 12 7	Copy of Medical Directory, 1871,	0 9 3
In Bank of Scotland on 5th January 1870, at credit of Scottish Branch Council,	487 17 3	Postal and Receipt-Stamps, and Registration of Letters,	3 16 6
In Consols, as formerly stated,	1907 10 0	Messengers, Telegrams, Parcels, and Miscellaneous Expenses,	0 5 6
140 Registration Fees at £5,	700 0 0	Printing (Constable),	2 15 0
5 Registration Fees at £2,	10 0 0	Stationery (Waterston),	0 5 0
62 Additional Qualifications, Registered at 5s.,	15 10 0	Clerk's Writings (J. J. M'Lachlan),	2 2 0
Dividend, January 1870, on £2000 Consols,	29 7 6	Auditor's Fee for last Account,	2 2 0
Dividend, July 1870, on do.	29 10 0	Registrar's Salary and Office-rent to 11th November 1870,	210 0 0
Interest allowed by Bank of Scotland on the Account of 1869,	5 17 11	Remitted, on Account of General Medical Council, with Bank Commission,	611 14 0
Interest allowed by Bank of Scotland on the Account of 1870,	3 6 9	Fees and Travelling Expenses of Branch Councillors in 1870,	18 18 0
Sales of Medical Register in Edinburgh,	0 9 0	In Consols, as formerly stated,	1907 10 0
		In Bank of Scotland on 5th January 1871, at credit of Scottish Branch Council,	402 11 0
		Balance, being cash in Registrar's hands,	31 12 9
Sum of Charge,	£3194 1 0	Sum of Discharge,	£3194 1 0

EDINBURGH, 9th January 1871.—The undersigned having examined the above Account, finds it correctly stated and duly vouched.

It is suggested that the sum invested in Consols, which stands in the names of Mr. Syme and Dr. Christison, should, in consequence of Mr. Syme's death, be transferred to the names of Dr. Christison and Dr. Andrew Wood, the existing Treasurers.

THOS. G. DICKSON, C.A., *Auditor*.

STATEMENT by the TREASURERS OF SCOTTISH BRANCH MEDICAL COUNCIL of GROSS RECEIPTS, from 5th January 1870 to 5th January 1871.

	£ s. d.
140 Registration Fees at £5; 5 do. at £2; 62 Additional do. at 5s.,	725 10 0
Dividends, January 1870, £29, 7s. 6d.; and July 1870, £29, 10s., on £2000 Consols,	58 17 6
Interest, accruing on Bank Account, in 1869, £5, 17s. 11d.; in 1870, £3, 6s. 9d.,	9 4 8
Sales of Medical Register,	0 9 0
Gross Receipts of Scottish Branch Council,	£794 1 2

R. CHRISTISON,
ANDREW WOOD, } *Treasurers*.

(No. 60.)

SCOTTISH BRANCH

OF THE

GENERAL COUNCIL

OF

MEDICAL EDUCATION & REGISTRATION.

Physicians' Hall, Edinburgh,
23d June 1871.

Sederunt—

Dr. Macrobin, *Chairman.*

Dr. Christison.   Dr. Fleming.   Dr. Andrew Wood.

Dr. Alexander Wood.   Dr. Allen Thomson.

Dr. William Robertson, *Registrar.*

---

1. The Minutes of last Meeting were read and confirmed.

2. *Read*—Official announcement of the re-appointment of Dr. Sharpey as a Member of the General Medical Council.

3. *Read*—Communication from the Secretary of the Royal College of Physicians of Edinburgh in reference to the case of Mr. David Gibb. After taking the advice of counsel, the Royal College had agreed to the following Resolution :—"That the College take no active proceedings against Mr. Gibb with the view of depriving him of his License, and that this Resolution be communicated to the Scottish Branch of the General Medical

Council, together with a copy of the Queries submitted to the Solicitor-General, and of his opinion thereon."

4. *Read*—Petition from Mr. W. H. WOODBURN requesting exemption from the Regulations as to Student Registration.

The Branch Council declined to make any special order in this case.

5. *Read*—Petition from Mr. AUSTIN E. MEHAMS requesting relaxation of the Regulations as to Student Registration.

The Branch Council declined to make any special order in reference to this case.

6. *Read*—Petition from Mr. GAVIN requesting that the Royal College of Physicians of Edinburgh might be authorised in his case to accept the certificate of Matriculation at Harvard College, in lieu of evidence of Medical Registration or preliminary Examination.

It was agreed that the Royal College should be authorised to proceed in this and in similar cases according to its own laws, and in conformity with the spirit of the Medical Council's Recommendations.

7. *Read*—Petition from Mr. JAMES LITTLE.

It was agreed that Mr. LITTLE'S Medical Studies should be held as having commenced on 1st November 1870.

8. *Read*—Petition from Mr. D. C. DAVIDSON.

It was agreed that Mr. DAVIDSON'S Medical Studies should be held to have commenced on 1st November 1868.

9. *Read*—Petition from Mr. T. D. F. EVANS.

It was agreed that Mr. EVANS'S Medical Studies should be held to have commenced on 1st April 1870.

10. *Read*—Petition from Mr. JOHN CRAVEN.

It was agreed that Mr. CRAVEN'S Medical Studies should be held to have commenced in April 1870.

Confirmed—J. MACROBIN.

No. 61.

SCOTTISH BRANCH

OF THE

GENERAL COUNCIL

OF

MEDICAL EDUCATION & REGISTRATION.

PHYSICIANS' HALL, EDINBURGH,
27th December 1871.

Sederunt—

Dr. FLEMING, *Chairman.*

SIR ROBERT CHRISTISON, Bart.   Dr. ALLEN THOMSON.
    Dr. ANDREW WOOD.   Dr. ALEXANDER WOOD.
        Dr. MACROBIN.
Dr. WILLIAM ROBERTSON, *Registrar.*

---

1. The Minutes of last Meeting were read and confirmed.

2. *Read*—An application by Mr. JOHN A. FORBES, of 33 West North Street, Aberdeen, relative to the disposal of the sum of £9, 19s. 3d., being the amount of penalties for infraction of the provisions of the Medical Act, recovered at Aberdeen from an irregular practitioner named Chadwick, and which had been paid over to the Treasurer of the General Medical Council.

After considering correspondence relative to this subject, the Branch Council resolved :—That the Treasurer of the General Medical Council be instructed to contribute the amount of money penalty recovered from Chadwick, or such portion of it as may defray the legal expenses of the case, to the prosecutor, Mr. JOHN A. FORBES of Aberdeen.

3. *Read*—Petition from Mr. COLIN MUNRO MACANDREW.

It was agreed that Mr. MACANDREW'S Medical Studies should be held as having commenced on 1st November 1870.

4. *Read*—Petition from Mr. ROBERT ANDERSON.

It was agreed that Mr. ANDERSON'S Medical Studies should be held as having commenced on 1st November 1870.

5. *Read*—Petition from Mr. H. M. LECHLER.

It was agreed that Mr. LECHLER'S Medical Studies should be held as having commenced on 1st November 1869.

6. *Read*—Petition from Mr. JAMES COMPTON BURNETT.

It was agreed that Mr. BURNETT, having commenced Medical Study in 1865, is exempt from the obligation of becoming registered as a Medical Student.

7. *Read*—Petition from Mr. GEORGE HOGGAN.

It was agreed that Mr. HOGGAN'S Medical Studies should be held as having commenced on 3d October 1868.

8. *Read*—Petition from Mr. D. C. DAVIDSON.

It was agreed that, as regards the recognition of Mr. DAVIDSON'S Medical Studies, the Branch Council adhere to their Minutes of 23d June 1871.

9. *Read*—Petition from Mr. ALEXANDER BOMERBANK CAMPBELL.

It was agreed that Mr. CAMPBELL'S Medical Studies should be held as having commenced in August 1867.

10. It was agreed that a gratuity of Five Guineas be paid to the Officer of the Royal College of Physicians of Edinburgh, for

services rendered to the Branch Council in connexion with their Meetings.

11. It was agreed that the Annual Accounts of the Branch Council should be prepared on 1st January 1872; that they should be audited, as formerly, by THOS. G. DICKSON, Esq., C.A.; that they should be circulated after audit along with the Confidential Copies of these Minutes; and that a note of the Gross Receipts of the Branch Council during 1871 should be sent as soon as possible to the Registrar of the General Medical Council.

Confirmed—J. G. FLEMING.

Dec. 27, 1871.] SCOTTISH BRANCH COUNCIL. 9

ACCOUNT, Charge and Discharge, of the TREASURERS' Intromissions with the FUNDS of the SCOTTISH BRANCH OF GENERAL MEDICAL COUNCIL, from 5th January 1871 to 1st January 1872.

CHARGE.		DISCHARGE.	
Balance, Cash in Registrar's hands, on 5th January 1871,	£31 12 9	Postal and Receipt Stamps, and Registration of Letters,	£4 7 0
In Bank of Scotland on 5th January 1871, at credit of Scottish Branch Council,	402 11 0	Messengers, and Miscellaneous Petty Expenses,	0 12 6
		Printing (Constable),	2 9 6
		Stationery (Waterston),	1 13 0
In Consols, as formerly stated,	1907 10 0	Clerk's Writings (Mr. Baird),	2 10 0
117 Registration Fees at £5,	585 0 0	Auditor's Fee for last Account,	2 2 0
8 Registration Fees at £2,	16 0 0	Registrar's Salary and Office-rent to 11th November 1871,	210 0 0
49 Additional Qualifications, Registered at 5s.,	12 5 0	Remitted, on Account of General Medical Council, with Bank Commission,	510 3 10
Dividend, January 1871, on £2000 Consols,	29 10 0	Fees and Travelling Expenses of Branch Councillors in 1871,	45 3 0
Dividend, July 1871, on do.,	29 5 0	Gratuity to Officer (Marshall) at Royal College of Physicians,	5 5 0
Interest on Account of 1871 with the Bank of Scotland,	2 12 9	In Consols, as formerly stated,	1907 10 0
Sales of Medical Register in Edinburgh,	0 8 0	In Bank of Scotland on 1st January 1872, at credit of Scottish Branch Council,	321 0 2
		Balance, being cash in Registrar's hands,	3 18 6
Sum of Charge,	£3016 14 6	Sum of Discharge,	£3016 14 6

EDINBURGH, 6th January 1872.—The undersigned having examined the above Account, finds it correctly stated and duly vouched.

The Sum invested in Consols still stands in names of the late Mr. Syme and of Sir Robert Christison. Reference is made to the Auditor's suggestion in the Doquet to last year's Account as to the expediency of having the Stock transferred to the names of the existing Treasurers.

THOS. G. DICKSON, C.A., *Auditor.*

STATEMENT by the TREASURERS OF SCOTTISH BRANCH MEDICAL COUNCIL of GROSS RECEIPTS, from 5th January 1871 to 1st January 1872.

117 Registration Fees at £5; 8 do. at £2; 49 Additional do. at 5s.,	£613 5 0
Dividend, January 1871, £29, 10s.; and July 1871, £29, 5s., on £2000 Consols,	58 15 0
Interest on Bank Account of 1871,	2 12 9
Sales of Medical Register,	0 8 0
Gross Receipts of Scottish Branch Council,	£675 0 9

b

IRISH BRANCH OF GENERAL COUNCIL

OF

MEDICAL EDUCATION AND REGISTRATION.

MINUTES OF MEETING, FRIDAY, MARCH 10, 1871.

Present

CHARLES H. LEET, M. D., in the Chair.

SIR D. J. CORRIGAN, Bart., M. P. AQUILLA SMITH, M. D.
JAMES APJOHN, M. D. WILLIAM HARGRAVE, M. B.

W. E. STEELE, M. D., *Registrar*.

The Minutes of the last Meeting were read and signed.

The Requisition convening the present Meeting was signed by Sir D. J. CORRIGAN, Bart., Dr. SMITH, and Dr. HARGRAVE.

The Summary of the Accounts of this Branch Council for the year ending 5th January, 1871, duly audited, was submitted.

RESOLVED,—That the Summary of the Account now submitted be appended to the Minutes of the present Meeting.

The Statement of Accounts of the General and Branch Councils, as printed in the Minutes of the Executive Committee of the 24th February, 1871, whereby it appears that the percentage rate due by this Branch Council for the year ending 5th January last, amounts to £714 13s. 9d., having been submitted,

RESOLVED,—That the percentage rate, amounting to £714 13s. 9d., be paid; and that so much 3 per cent. stock as will produce £100 net, be sold.

(Signed) CHAS. H. LEET, M. D.,
Chairman.

May 24, 1871.

SUMMARY OF ACCOUNT OF THE BRANCH MEDICAL COUNCIL (IRELAND).

For the Year ending 5th January, 1871.

CHARGE.

1870.		£	s.	d.
Jan. 5th.	To Balance in favour of the Council at foot of last Year's Account, ...	479	8	4
October 8th.	,, Amount of One Year's dividend on £2241 2s. 2d., Govt. New 3 per cent. Stock (less Income Tax, £1 5s. 3d.), ...	65	19	5
1871. Jan. 5th.	,, Amount of Registration Fees to date, viz.:			
	205 Registrations, at £5 0 0 .. £1025 0 0			
	2 do. at 2 0 0 .. 4 0 0			
	73 do. at 0 5 0 .. 18 5 0	1047	5	0
	Total, ..	£1592	12	9

DISCHARGE.

1870.		£	s.	d.
April 12th.	By Amount paid Proportion of Expenses of General Council, for the Year ending 5th January, 1870,	713	5	8
Nov. 10th.	,, Amount paid One Year's Rent of Office, to date, ..	36	0	0
,, 24th.	,, Amount paid Registrar, One Year's Salary, to date,	200	0	0
Dec. 22nd.	,, Amount paid Councillor's Fees, for Meetings of 1st and 15th April and 22nd December, 1870, ..	33	12	0
1871. Jan. 5th.	,, Amount of Postage and Receipt Stamps, to date,	4	0	0
,, ,,	,, Amount of Stationery, to date, ...	4	8	10
,, ,,	,, Amount of Printing, to date, ...	8	0	0
,, ,,	,, Amount of Incidental Office Expenses, to date, ..	1	16	0
,, ,,	Balance in Bank on 3rd Jan., 1871, £576 14 6 Cash in Registrar's hands, on 5th inst., 14 15 9	591	10	3
	Total, ..	£1592	12	9

We have examined the Account of the Branch Medical Council for Ireland, and carefully checked the Vouchers, and hereby certify the above to be a correct Statement of the same; and that the Balance to the credit of the Council on the Fifth day of January, 1871 (seventy-one), amounts to Five Hundred and Ninety-one Pounds Ten Shillings and Three Pence.

Dated this Sixth day of January, 1871 (seventy-one).

(Signed) AQUILLA SMITH, M.D., *Treasurer,*
CHARLES HENRY LEET, M.D., } *Auditors.*

(No. 73.)

IRISH BRANCH OF GENERAL COUNCIL

OF

MEDICAL EDUCATION AND REGISTRATION.

MINUTES OF MEETING, WEDNESDAY, MAY 24, 1871.

Present—

CHARLES H. LEET, M.D., in the Chair.

SIR D. J. CORRIGAN, BART., M.P.   WILLIAM STOKES, M.D.
JAMES APJOHN, M.D.   WILLIAM HARGRAVE, M.B.
AQUILLA SMITH, M.D.

W. E. STEELE, M.D., *Registrar.*

The Minutes of the last Meeting were read and signed.

The Requisition convening the present Meeting was signed by Sir D. J. CORRIGAN, Bart. and Dr. SMITH.

The attention of the Council having been directed to the Report of an "Inquest on a Lady," as published in the "Freeman's Journal," of May 22, 1871, it was

RESOLVED—That the Registrar be directed to send a copy of the following letter to the Editor of the "Freeman's Journal," for publication in that newspaper:—

"TO THE EDITOR OF THE FREEMAN'S JOURNAL.

"BRANCH MEDICAL COUNCIL (IRELAND).
"35, *Dawson-street, May* 24, 1871.

"SIR.—The attention of the Branch Medical Council for Ireland has been drawn to the report of 'An Inquest on a Lady,' in your paper of Monday, 22nd instant, in which there is the following paragraph:—

"'Dr. William Ledger Erson, examined—I reside at 39, Henry-street, I knew the deceased lady. * * * I was her Medical Attendant * * * I am a Physician of the College of New York, but I never was in that city. I am registered here only as an Accoucheur.'

"In reference thereto I am directed to state that the name of 'William Ledger Erson' does not appear in the Medical Register of 'legally or duly qualified medical practitioners' of the United Kingdom, in either 'medicine,' 'surgery,' or 'midwifery;' and I am further directed, for the information and protection of the public, to note the following sections of the Medical Act of 1858, xxi. and xxii. Vict. cap. xc.

"By sect. xxxii. it is enacted that—

"'No person * * * shall be entitled to recover any charge in any court of law for any medical or surgical advice, attendance, or for the performance of any operation, or for any medicine which he shall have both prescribed and supplied, unless he shall prove upon the trial that he is registered under this Act.'

"By sect. xxxvii. it is enacted that—

"'No certificate * * * from any physician, surgeon, licentiate in medicine and surgery, or other medical practitioner shall be valid unless the person signing the same be registered under this Act.'

"And by sect. xl. it is enacted that—

"'Any person who shall wilfully and falsely pretend * * * that he is recognized by law as a physician or surgeon, or licentiate in medicine and surgery, or a practitioner in medicine, or an apothecary, shall upon a summary conviction for any such offence, pay a sum not exceeding twenty pounds.'

"I am, Sir, your obedient Servant,
"W. E. STEELE, M.D., Registrar.

"P.S.—The 'Medical Register' is published annually under the Act of Parliament xxi. and xxii. Vict. c. xc., and is furnished to all courts of law, to chairmen of quarter sessions, to coroners, &c."

(Signed)   D. J. CORRIGAN,
Chairman.

May 30, 1871.

(No. 74.)

IRISH BRANCH OF GENERAL COUNCIL
OF
MEDICAL EDUCATION AND REGISTRATION.

MINUTES OF MEETING, TUESDAY, MAY 30, 1871.

Present:

SIR D. J. CORRIGAN, BART., M.P., in the Chair.

AQUILLA SMITH, M. D.   WM. STOKES, M. D.
WM. HARGREAVE, M. B.   CHAS. H. LEET, M. D.

W. E. STEELE, M. D., *Registrar.*

The Minutes of the last Meeting were read and signed.

The Requisition convening the present Meeting was signed by Sir D. J. CORRIGAN, Bart., and Dr. SMITH.

READ,—The following letter published in the "Freeman's Journal," of the 26th instant, and in other Dublin Morning Newspapers, viz. :—

"THE EXTRAORDINARY INQUEST ON A LADY.

"SIR,—In reference to a letter signed "Wm. Steele," of this day, I beg to state—that I hold the medical diploma as mentioned in my evidence on the inquest to which he refers, and that my diploma for midwifery was granted by the Coombe Hospital (which is incorporated by Royal Charter), on the 12th of September, 1868, under the hands and seals of Doctors Jemison, Churchill, Wilmot, Banks, Porter, Ringland, and Sawyer, and that my name appears in the return of qualified Medical Practitioners in Midwifery—published annually by the Hospital.—I am, yours, &c.

"WM. LEDGER ERSON.

"39, *Henry-street, May* 25*th*, 1871."

RESOLVED,—That a letter be addressed to each of the Gentlemen named in the letter signed W. L. Erson, which appeared in the "Freeman's Journal," and other Morning Papers of 26th May, requesting his attention to it, and asking him to have the kindness, if not inconvenient to him, to meet the Branch Medical Council on Tuesday next, 6th June, at 4 o'clock P.M., to consider what further steps, if any, should be taken in the matter, as the Branch Medical Council are desirous to adopt such measures as may seem requisite for the protection of the Public and the maintenance of the position of the Profession.

RESOLVED,—That a letter be written to the Registrar of the Coombe Lying-in Hospital, enclosing a copy of Mr. W. L. Erson's letter as published in the Morning Papers of 26th instant, and requesting he will have the kindness to forward to the Branch Medical Council, on or before Saturday, June 3, a copy of the Charter of the Hospital, and of the Diploma issued by the Hospital authorities.

    (Signed) WM. HARGRAVE,
             Chairman.

June 10, 1871.

IRISH BRANCH OF GENERAL COUNCIL

OF

MEDICAL EDUCATION AND REGISTRATION.

MINUTES OF MEETING, SATURDAY, JUNE 10, 1871.

Present:

WILLIAM HARGRAVE, M. B., in the Chair.

AQUILLA SMITH, M. D.　　SIR D. J. CORRIGAN, Bart., M. P.
JAMES APJOHN, M. D.　　CHARLES H. LEET, M. D.

W. E. STEELE, M. D., *Registrar.*

The Minutes of the last Meeting were read and signed.

The present Meeting was held instead of that to have taken place on the 6th instant, but which was unavoidably postponed.

The following gentlemen were, in accordance with the resolution passed at the last Meeting, present, viz.:—Dr. BANKS, Dr. JAMESON, Dr. CHURCHILL, Dr. SAWYER, Mr. PORTER.

A copy of the Charter and By-Laws of the Coombe Lying-in Hospital, which contains the Form of Certificate granted by the Hospital authorities was submitted, when the following memorandum was agreed to and submitted to the Branch Council:—

MEMORANDUM.

In reference to the letter of Mr. William Ledger Erson, published in the "Freeman's Journal," of the 26th May last, we desire to state that Certificates issued from Lying-in Hospitals do not make persons who obtain such Certificates "qualified Medical Practitioners in Midwifery;" and that such Certificates are merely documents showing that such persons, whether male or female, as have obtained them, have duly attended the Lectures and practice of such Hospitals, and have satisfied the Master or Masters of said Hospitals of their proficiency in Midwifery, and the diseases of women and children.

                              J. H. SAWYER, M. D.,
                         One of the Masters of the Coombe Lying-in Hospital.

(Signed)   WM. JAMESON, M. D., } *Consulting*
                    F. CHURCHILL,   } *Accoucheurs.*

                     J. T. BANKS, *Consulting Physician.*

                     GEO. H. PORTER, *Consulting Surgeon.*

June 10, 1871.

      (Signed)   AQUILLA SMITH, M. D.
June 21, 1871.

IRISH BRANCH OF GENERAL COUNCIL

OF

MEDICAL EDUCATION AND REGISTRATION.

MINUTES OF MEETING, WEDNESDAY, JUNE 21, 1871.

Present:

AQUILLA SMITH, M. D., in the Chair.

SIR D. J. CORRIGAN, BART., M. P.   AQUILLA SMITH, M. D.
WILLIAM HARGRAVE, M. B.   CHARLES H. LEET, M. D.

W. E. STEELE, M. D., *Registrar*.

The Minutes of the last Meeting were read and signed.

The Council having taken into consideration the Memorandum signed by certain of the Medical Officers of the Coombe Lying-in Hospital, Dublin, as entered in the Minutes of the last Meeting, it was

RESOLVED—That the following letter be addressed by the Registrar to the Poor Law Commissioners, Ireland :—

"BRANCH MEDICAL COUNCIL (IRELAND).

"35, *Dawson-street, June* 22, 1871.

"SIR,—I am directed by this Branch Council to acquaint you for the information of the Commissioners for administering the laws for relief of the poor in Ireland that it has come to the knowledge of this Council that a 'Certificate in Midwifery,' recognised by your Board, and required from Candidates for Poor Law appointments, in addition to a Medical and Surgical Degree or License, has been used by persons not legally qualified in Medicine or Surgery, to impose themselves upon the public as qualified practitioners, and that the fact of its being so recognised and required by your Board has aided such persons in the imposition.

"The passage in the Poor Law regulations to which I beg to draw your attention, is the following:—

* * * 'And also a Certificate from some Board or Court of Examiners, or other body duly authorized to grant the same, of his possessing a competent knowledge of Midwifery.'

"In reference to the above, I am directed to observe that no Certificate or Diploma in Midwifery issued in Ireland is recognised as a legal qualification, or entitled to be registered under the Medical Act of 1858, except issued on due examination by the University of Dublin, the Queen's University, the King's and Queen's College of Physicians, Ireland, or the Royal College of Surgeons, Ireland, and your Board would therefore seem to be unadvisedly recognising as a legal qualification what is not recognised by law.

"In the year 1859, memorials were presented to the General Medical Council from the authorities of the Dublin Lying-in Hospital, Rotunda, and the Coombe Lying-in Hospital, Dublin, requesting that their Certificates should be received as qualifications for registration.

"To this the following was the reply :—

"'That in reference to the Memorials of the Governors of the Lying-in Hospital, in Dublin, and of the Coombe Lying-in Hospital, in Dublin, it is not in the power of this Council to comply with them.'—[*Vide* Minutes of General Medical Council of Meeting of 4th August, 1859], Vol. i., p. 36.

"I am to observe that the Poor Law Boards of England and Scotland do not require special Certificates in Midwifery from Candidates for Poor Law appointments.

"The present regulations of your Board, which require both a Medical and Surgical Degree or License from Candidates for Poor Law appointments, insure a knowledge of Midwifery, as the joint Degrees or Licenses in Medicine and Surgery cannot be obtained without examination in Midwifery. This Council would, therefore, suggest to the Poor Law

Commissioners of Ireland the propriety of rescinding the regulation referred to.

"If, however, the Commissioners should still think it necessary to require a special Diploma in Midwifery from Candidates holding both Medical and Surgical qualifications, this Council would submit for the consideration of the Poor Law Commissioners that they should only recognise as a Midwifery qualification from any body in Ireland what is legally so, viz., the Diploma in Midwifery from the University of Dublin, the Queen's University, Ireland, the King's and Queen's College of Physicians, and the Royal College of Surgeons of Ireland.

" I am directed to send for your information the enclosed copies of Minutes of the Meetings of the Branch Medical Council (Ireland) of 24th and 30th May last, and 20th June inst.

" *To* B. BANKS, ESQ., *Chief Clerk*,
" *Poor Law Commissioners, Dublin.*"

RESOLVED,—That the fees due to the Members of this Branch Council for attendance at the Meetings of the 30th May last, and 10th and 21st June instant, be paid.

(Signed) D. J. CORRIGAN, BART.,
Chairman.

Feb. 5, 1872.

STANDING ORDERS & REGULATIONS

OF THE

GENERAL MEDICAL COUNCIL.

1872

CONTENTS.

		PAGE
I.	Meetings of the General Council	3
II.	Forms to be observed on the Introduction of New Members of the Council	ib.
III.	Order of Business	4
IV.	Minutes of the Councils	5
V.	Committees	6
VI.	Executive Committee	ib.
VII.	Registration	8
VIII.	Removal of a Name from the Register	11
IX.	Fees for Registration	12
X.	Fees for attending Councils	13
XI.	Treasurers	14
XII.	Registrar	ib.
XIII.	Penalties	15
XIV.	Appointment of Members of the Council	ib.
XV.	Corporate Seal	16

STANDING ORDERS & REGULATIONS

OF

THE GENERAL MEDICAL COUNCIL.

I.

MEETINGS OF THE GENERAL COUNCIL.

1. That the President, or any eight Members of the General Council, may summon a Meeting of the General Council at any time, by letter addressed to each Member.—(Minutes, vol. i., p. 21.)

2. That previously to any Session or Special Meeting of the General Council, the Registrar prepare a Programme of Business, and furnish two copies to each Member of the Council, not less than three days before the day of Meeting.—(Minutes, vol. ii., p. 4.)

II.

FORMS TO BE OBSERVED ON THE INTRODUCTION OF NEW MEMBERS OF THE COUNCIL.

1. That the President, on receiving intimation of the resignation or death of any Member of the General Medical Council, cause notice of the same to be sent to the Registrar of each of the Branch Councils.—(Minutes, vol. i., p. 154.)

2. That the President, on receiving from any of the Bodies entitled to send representatives to the Medical Council, or in the case of Members nominated by the Crown, an official notice of the election or nomination of a new Member or of new Members, announce the same to the Registrar of each Branch Council.—(*Ibid.*)

3. That the Registrar summon the person so elected or nominated to the first Meeting of the Branch Council to be held after such announcement; and that before the new Member presents himself at such Meeting, the President's notification of his election or nomination be read, and that he be then introduced to the Meeting by some Member of the Branch Council.—(Minutes, vol. i., p. 154.)

4. That the same forms be observed in the case of Members who have or have not taken their seat in the Branch Council, when they take their seat for the first time in the General Council.—(*Ibid.*)

III.
ORDER OF BUSINESS.

1. That the Council meet each day at 2 o'clock p.m., and do not sit after 6 p.m.—(Minutes, vol i., p. 30.)

2. That the hour of Meeting of the Council shall be 1 p.m., and of adjournment 4 p.m., when the Meetings shall take place on Saturdays.—(Minutes, vol. iv., p. 8.)

3. That the roll be called on the President's taking the Chair, and that any Member not present before the Minutes of the previous day are confirmed, be deemed absent.—(Minutes, vol. ii., p. 8.)

4. That no Member, after taking his place, leave the Meeting without the permission of the Chairman.—(*Ibid.*)

5. That during the Sessions of the Council, a Programme of subjects to be brought forward, and of notices of Motions given by Members, be prepared, printed, and distributed by the Registrar from day to day, as may be required, and that a Committee be annually appointed to aid the Registrar in this matter.—(Minutes, vol. ii., p. 5.)

6. That any Motion or Motions lying over from the previous day take precedence of new matter, except by special permission of the Council.—(Minutes, vol. i., p. 43.)

7. That no Motion or Amendment be withdrawn after having been put from the Chair, except by leave of the Meeting.—(Minutes, vol. ii., p. 5.)

8. That the Seconder of a Motion may, if he pleases, reserve his Speech.—(Minutes, vol. iii., p. 17.)

9. That if an Amendment be proposed on a Motion, the Amendment be disposed of before any other Amendment shall be moved.—(Minutes, vol. iii., p. 18.)

10. That such Amendment be first put to the vote; that if it be negatived, a second Amendment may be moved, and shall be disposed of in the same way as the first Amendment; and so on until no further Amendment shall be proposed.—(*Ibid.*)

11. That should every Amendment be negatived, the original Motion be then put to the vote.—(*Ibid.*)

12. That if any Amendment be carried, it be then put as a substantive Motion, and treated, as to further Amendments, and the right of speaking on it, in all respects as an original Motion.—(*Ibid.*)

13. That all Amendments be so framed that they may be read as independent Motions.—(Minutes, vol. ii., p. 5.)

14. That in all cases where a division has taken place, any Member of the Council may require that the Names or Numbers of the Majority and Minority, and of those declining to vote, be entered on the Minutes.—(Minutes, vol. iii., p. 78.)

15. *Mode of procedure in the case of Motions having reference to any* PENAL MEASURES.

    1. That the deliberations of the Council between the completion of the evidence and the decision of the case be held in private.

    2. That the question, as to the person charged being guilty or not guilty, be put from the Chair, and not in the form of Resolution by Mover and Seconder.—(Minutes G. C., March 5th, 1872, p. 65, § 5.)

IV.

MINUTES OF THE COUNCILS.

1. That the proceedings of the Meetings of the General Council

be recorded by the Registrar in writing, in a book to be kept for that purpose.—(Minutes, vol. i., p. 67.)

2. That the Minutes of each Meeting (marked "*Confidential*" until confirmed) be printed in 8vo., and sent to each Member from day to day.—(Minutes, vol. i., p. 3.)

3. That the Minutes of each Meeting contain such Motions and Amendments as have been proposed and adopted, or negatived, with the names of the Proposer and Seconder, and without any comment or observation of Members annexed.—(Minutes, vol. i., p. 6.)

4. That the Minutes of the Meetings of the Branch Councils, and of the Executive Committee, be printed uniformly with those of the General Council, and that copies of them (marked "*Confidential*") be sent to every Member of the General Council.—(Minutes, vol. i., p. 22.)

5. That after the close of any Session or Special Meeting of the Councils, two copies of the confirmed Minutes be sent to each Member.—(Minutes, vol. i., p. 23.)

V.

COMMITTEES.

1. That the President be *ex officio* a Member of all Committees.—(Minutes, vol. ii., p. 7.)

2. That no Report from any Committee of the Council shall appear in the Minutes until it has first been printed in the "Programme of Business."—(Minutes, vol. iv., p. 299.)

VI.

EXECUTIVE COMMITTEE.

1. That the Executive Committee make up the Annual Accounts, and compute the per-centage chargeable against each Branch Council.—(Minutes, vol. i., p. 71.)

2. That the Executive Committee keep regular written Minutes of their proceedings, and that these Minutes be printed, and circulated among the Members of the Council.—(Minutes, vol. i., p. 72.)

3. That the 5th of January in each year be the day on or

before which the Treasurers of Branch Councils shall make their Returns to the General Council; and that as soon thereafter as may be, the computation of the per-centage and amount of contributions of the Branch Councils be made, under Section XIII. of the Medical Act (lines 11 to 14 inclusive); and also that the Accounts of the General and Branch Councils be examined by the Executive Committee previously to their being laid before Parliament in the month of March, under Section XLIV. of the Act.—(Minutes, vol. i., p. 17.)

4. That in striking the annual per-centage rate, in accordance with Section XIII. of the Act, the words " all moneys received " be understood to mean all moneys received by the respective Branch Councils, from whatever sources derived.—(Minutes, vol. i., p. 151.)

5. That in the event of a vacancy, or vacancies, occurring during the recess, in the Executive Committee, they be empowered to fill up such vacancy or vacancies.—(Minutes, vol. i., p. 156.)

6. That the publication of the Register be superintended by the Executive Committee.—(Minutes, vol. i., p. 21.)

7. That it be delegated to the Executive Committee to print annually, in the Register, a statement of the distribution of the copies of the Register, as approved by the Government.—(Minutes, vol. ii., p. 204.)

8. That the Members of the Executive Committee be elected by Ballot, by means of Marked Lists.—(Minutes, vol. iii., p. 19.)

9. That the Executive Committee consist of six Members exclusive of the President, instead of four, as at present. That of the six Members to be elected, four be chosen from the English, one from the Scottish, and one from the Irish Branch Council.—(Minutes, vol. iv., p. 302.)

10. That it be delegated to the Executive Committee, in case of the death or incapacity from illness of the Registrar, when the General Council is not in session, to appoint a person to perform temporarily the duties of Registrar.—(Minutes, vol. iii., p. 307.)

11. That it be delegated to the Executive Committee to prepare annually, and lay before the Council for recognition, a list of Examining Bodies whose examinations shall fulfil the conditions of the Medical Council as regards Preliminary Education.—(Minutes, vol. iv., pp. 145-6.)

12. That the Executive Committee should consider and prepare Reports upon any subjects that may suggest themselves to them as requiring the attention of the General Council.—(Minutes, vol. v., p. 179.)

13. That such Reports should be printed and circulated among the Members of the General Council, at least one fortnight before its meeting.—(*Ibid.*)

14. That the Branch Councils be requested to transmit to the Executive Committee the Reports of the Visitations of Examinations, at least a month before the meeting of the General Council, in order that they may be printed, and circulated confidentially among the Members of Council.—(Minutes, vol. v., p. 180.)

15. That the Executive Committee meet before the annual Meeting of the General Council, in order to prepare and arrange the business for the consideration of the Council.—(*Ibid.*)

16. That the Executive Committee be authorized to apply to the Licensing Bodies for such information as may be necessary for the due execution by the Committee of such business as may be delegated to them.—(Minutes, vol. v., p. 256.)

17. That the printing of the Volumes of Minutes be under the direction of the Executive Committee.—(Minutes, vol. viii., pp. 17, 18.)

18. That the Returns from the Bodies in Schedule (A) of Professional Examinations and their Results be confided to the care of the Executive Committee.—(Minutes G. C., March 5th, 1872, pp. 63, 64, § 3).

VII.

REGISTRATION.

1. That the Register be made out in strict conformity with

Schedule (D) to the Medical Act, setting forth the name in the first column, the residence in the second, and the qualification in the third.—(Minutes, vol. i., p. 19.)

2. That the words "or any qualification" in Section XXX., line 2, be held to mean any of the "qualifications" mentioned in Schedule (A), and none other.—(Minutes, vol. i., p. 21.)

3. That a Foreign Degree, conferred without examination at the seat of the University or College granting such Degree, does not furnish sufficient reason for Registration."—(Minutes, vol. i., p. 34.)

4. That in every instance in which application shall have been made to register a Foreign or Colonial Degree, the Registrar of the General Council inquire, by letter addressed to the University or College which is represented to have conferred it, whether the name of the person making the application is really on its list; and if the degree or diploma has been conferred after examination by, and at the seat of, the University or College, and the date thereof. Also, that the Registrar, when communicating with Foreign or Colonial Universities and Colleges, shall endeavour to ascertain, in the case of each University or College, what examinations and conditions have been held by it to be indispensable for the admission of persons to Degrees or Diplomas in Medicine; and how far such examinations or conditions have been at any time, or under any circumstances, dispensed with or modified, in favour of persons who have not studied in the University or College in question.—(Minutes, vol. i., p. 25.)

5. That the General Registrar forward to each Branch Registrar the Returns received from the Foreign and Colonial Universities and Colleges, in answer to the circulars regarding applicants residing in his district; and that the Branch Registrars, under direction of the Branch Councils, enter on the Register the names of those Foreign and Colonial Graduates who appear from the Returns to have taken their Degrees after regular examination.—(Minutes, vol. i., p. 26.)

6. That the Branch Councils of England, Scotland, and Ireland respectively be empowered, under the Act (Section VI.), to direct the Registration, under the Act (Section XLVI.), of any persons who have held appointments as Surgeons or Assistant-Surgeons in the Army, Navy, or Militia, or in the service of the East India Company, or who were acting as Surgeons in the Public Service, or in the service of any Charitable Institution, on or before the 1st of October, 1858, after the production of evidence, satisfactory to the Branch Council to which such applications may be made, that there is sufficient ground for directing such registration to be made.—(Minutes, vol. i., p. 26.)

7. That when any person entitled to be registered under the Medical Act applies to the Registrar of any of the Branch Councils for that purpose, such Registrar forthwith enter in a Local Register, in the form set forth in Schedule (D) to the Act, or to the like effect, to be kept by him for that purpose, the name and place of residence, and the qualification, or several qualifications, in respect of which the person is so entitled, and affix to such entry in the Register the date at which it was made.—(Minutes, vol. i., p. 63.)

8. That the Registrar of each Branch Council, within two clear days (Sundays excepted) after he has received notice of any alteration in the addresses or qualifications, or legal evidence of the death, of any person registered under the Act, cause corresponding alterations to be made in the Register, and the name of such deceased person to be erased from the Register.—(Minutes, vol. i., p. 64.)

9. That the Registrars of the Branch Councils for Scotland and Ireland keep an alphabetical list of persons registered; and, after entering a name in the Local Register, enter it forthwith also in its own place in the alphabetical list.—(*Ibid.*)

10. That, as provided by the Act (Section XXV.), the Registrar for Scotland or Ireland send, with all convenient speed, to the Registrar of the General Council, a copy, certified under his

hand, of all the changes so made in the Local Register.—
(*Ibid.*)

11. That the General Registrar forthwith cause such changes in the Branch Registers to be made in the General Register.—(*Ibid.*)

12. That the General Registrar also keep, as directed by the Act (Section XXVII.), the General Register in alphabetical order ; and on receiving any additional name, forthwith enter it in such General Register.—(Minutes, vol. i., p. 64.)

13. That each page of these Registers be verified by the signature of the Registrar.—(*Ibid.*)

14. That, in accordance with the recommendation of the Finance Committee, printed lists of new entries in the Local Registers be henceforth issued not oftener than once a quarter.—(Minutes, vol. ii., p. 123.)

15. That the quarterly Local Lists, authenticated by the Registrars of the Branch Councils, be transmitted in manuscript to the Registrar of the General Council, who shall cause the same to be printed in London, in the type and form used for the General Register, and copies to be sent to the Members of the Council.—(*Ibid.*)

VIII.

REMOVAL OF A NAME FROM THE REGISTER.

1. That any application for the removal of a name from the Register be investigated, in the first instance, by the Branch Council of that part of the Kingdom in which the person whose name is proposed to be removed may reside.—(Minutes, vol. ii., p. 54.)

2. That in the event of such an application being made to the Registrar of the General Council, the Registrar of the General Council refer the question to the Branch Council by whom it should, under the preceding Regulation, be primarily investigated. —(*Ibid.*)

3. That the Branch Council, having investigated the case, and having collected the evidence, send a statement of the case, and the evidence in support of it, to the Registrar of the General Council, one calendar month before the probable time of the meeting of the General Council.—(*Ibid.*)

4. That the Registrar of the General Council, under the direction of the President, consult the Solicitors of the General Council, and, if necessary, take Counsel's opinion on the case; and, if so directed, summon the person against whom the proceedings have been instituted to attend the General Council.—(Minutes, vol. ii., p. 54.)

5. That if the Solicitors or Counsel shall advise that the application is not tenable, or that the evidence is insufficient, the application be referred back to the Branch Council with whom the proceedings originated.—(*Ibid.*)

6. That, should the Council remove the name of any person from the Register under Section XXVIII. or XXIX. of the Medical Act, due intimation of the same be made to all the Bodies enumerated in Schedule (A) to the Act.—(Minutes, vol. ii., p. 54; and vol. iii., p. 80.)

7. That the Registrar be directed to send annually, within one month after the meeting of the Council, to the various Bodies in Schedule (A), the names of those who, during the Meeting of the Council, have been struck off the Register by order of the Council, and to request the attention of each Body to Regulation 8, Chapter VIII., of the Standing Orders.—(Minutes, vol. ii., p. 239.)

8. That the Council recommend, that any person whose name has been once removed from the Register shall not be admitted to examination for any new qualification without the consent of the General Medical Council.—(Minutes, vol. ii., p. 240.)

IX.

FEES FOR REGISTRATION.

1. That the following be the scale of fees payable for Registration, viz.:

2. For all persons qualified before the 1st of January, 1859, Two Pounds.

3. For all persons qualified after the 1st of January, 1859, Five Pounds.

4. For persons in practice before 1815, Two Pounds.

5. For the insertion of additional qualifications, Five Shillings.

(Minutes, vol. i., p. 7.)

X.

FEES FOR ATTENDING COUNCILS.

1. That the scale of fees adopted on the 3rd of August, 1859, for attendance on the General Council, the Executive Committee, and the Branch Councils, and also for travelling and hotel expenses, which was approved of by the Commissioners of Her Majesty's Treasury, be adhered to, until altered by the Council.—(Minutes, vol. i., p. 151.)

2. That the rate of payment for attendance on the General Council be the same for all Members of the Council.—(Minutes, vol. i., p. 29.)

3. That the fees for attendance on the General Council be Five Guineas per day to each Member attending.—(*Ibid.*)

4. That Members of the General Council residing at more than two hundred miles from London, shall receive Five Guineas per day for the day of their coming and for the day of their return. —(*Ibid.*)

5. That the travelling expenses be on the scale formerly approved of by the General Council, and that a Guinea a day be allowed to non-resident Members for hotel expenses.—(*Ibid.*)

6. That the fees for attendance at the Meetings of the Executive Committee and Branch Councils be Two Guineas to each Member attending, his travelling expenses being also paid.—(*Ibid.*)

Scale of Travelling Expenses.

	£	s.	d.
Scotland	9	9	0
Ireland	8	8	0
Newcastle	6	6	0
Southampton	2	2	0
Cambridge	2	2	0
Oxford	2	2	0

(*Ibid.*)

7. That the non-resident Members of the General Medical Council be paid hotel expenses for every Sunday while in London on the business of the Council.—(Minutes, vol. i., p. 151.)

8. That the Visitors of Examinations shall in future receive payment for their services, at the same rate as for attending a Meeting of the Branch Council, in addition to travelling expenses.—(Minutes, vol. v., p. 235.)

XI.

TREASURERS.

1. That two Members of the Council, resident in London, be Treasurers, and that all cheques on the Bank be signed by one of the Treasurers, and, in addition, by the Registrar.—(Minutes, vol. i., p. 15.)

XII.

REGISTRAR.

1. That the salary of the Registrar be fixed at £500 per annum.—(Minutes, vol. i., p. 14.)

2. That £200 of the General Registrar's salary of £500 be charged against the funds of the Branch Council for England.—(Minutes, vol. ii., p. 251.)

3. That the Registrar be not Treasurer.—(Minutes, vol. i., p. 10.)

4. That the Registrar do not retain in his hands more than £100, but lodge all moneys, as they accumulate, in the Bank of England, to the credit of "The General Council of Medical Education and Registration of the United Kingdom."—(Minutes, vol. i., p. 15.)

5. That in all cases where Returns are required by the Council

from the Bodies in Schedule (A) to the Act, the Registrar of the Council be directed to give notice to the several Bodies at least one month before such Returns have to be rendered.—(Minutes, vol. ii., p. 105.)

6. That Returns from the Licensing Bodies in Schedule (A) be made annually on the 1st of January, and in the subjoined form (*see* Minutes, vol. ii., p. 127), to the General Medical Council, stating the number and names of the Candidates who have passed their first as well as their second Examinations, and the number of those who have been rejected at the first and second Examinations respectively; and that the Registrar forward a sufficient number of Forms, with a notice of their being returned in due time.—(Minutes, vol. ii., p. 127.)

XIII.

PENALTIES.

1. That the Treasurer of the General Council may contribute, under the direction of the Branch Councils, any portion, or the whole, of any money penalty, which may accrue to the Council from a successful prosecution under this Act, towards defraying the expenses of such prosecution.—(Minutes, vol. i., p. 53.)

XIV.

APPOINTMENT OF MEMBERS OF THE COUNCIL.

1. That a book be kept, containing the names of the Members of the Council, the Bodies they represent, the date of appointment of each Member, the term for which he was appointed, and the date of the death or retirement of each Member; and that such book be regularly kept up, so as at once to show the period at which each of the Bodies having power to appoint should proceed to a new appointment, also the same particulars with regard to Members appointed by the Crown.—(Minutes, vol. ii., p. 245.)

2. That a Form for appointing Members be prepared, and sent by the Registrar to the Secretary of State (Lord President of the Privy Council?), and to each Body having power to appoint, two months before the expiration of the term of the existing appoint-

ment, so that the new appointment may be made to take effect from the day on which the old appointment shall expire.

Form of such Appointment.

We, the   in pursuance of the power given to us by the Medical Act, do hereby appoint   to be a Member of the General Council of Medical Education and Registration of the United Kingdom, for the term of   year   from the   day of   187
(Minutes, vol. ii., p. 245.)

XV.

CORPORATE SEAL.

1. That the Corporate Seal be kept in a box having two different locks. That the key of one lock be in the custody of the President, and that of the other in the custody of the Registrar.—(Minutes, vol. ii., p. 242.)

2. That the Seal be affixed only by order of the General Council, or, when the General Council is not sitting, by order of the Executive Committee of the General Council; its use by such Committee being limited to such acts as may be necessary to effectuate the powers delegated to it by the General Council.—(Minutes, vol. ii., p. 243.)

3. That any order for affixing the Seal state the object of its use, and be entered on the Minutes of the General Council, or of the Executive Committee, as the case may be.—(*Ibid.*)

INDEX.

Figures, without Letters prefixed, indicate the pages of the Minutes of the General Council.
The Letters prefixed to Figures, indicate respectively—
    Ex. C.   Minutes of the Executive Committee.
    E. Br.   ,, ,, Branch Council for England.
    S. Br.   ,, ,, Branch Council for Scotland.
    I. Br.   ,, ,, Branch Council for Ireland.
    Standing Orders and Regulations.

                                                                       PAGE

ACCOUNTS,—
    Annual Accounts and Balance Sheets, considered and referred
        to a Professional Accountant . . . (Ex. C.) 2, 5
    ,, Approved . . . . . . (Ex. C.) 5
    Letter from Accountants . . . . . (Ex. C.) 5
ACCOUNTS of Scottish Branch Council . . (S. Br.) 2-3, 8-9
  ,, of Irish Branch Council . . . (I. Br.) 1-2
ANDERSON, ROBERT, his Studies to be ante-dated . (S. Br.) 7
AUDITORS . . . . (E. Br.) 4
  ,, ... (S. Br.) 8

BENNETT, Dr., elected Treasurer 35
BOUGHTON, J. G., his Studies to be ante-dated . (E. Br.) 5
BURNETT, J. C., his Studies to be ante-dated . (S. Br.) 7
BUSINESS COMMITTEE, appointed. 2
  ,,   ,, Thanks to Chairman . . . 54

CAMPBELL, A. B., his Studies to be ante-dated . . (S. Br.) 7
CAPE OF GOOD HOPE, Application from the Board of Public
    Examiners referred to a Committee 15
    Report of Committee, adopted 31
CHURCHILL, Dr. J. F., to be registered as M.D., Paris, 1848. (E. Br.) 4
CONJOINT EXAMINING BOARDS,—
    Dr. Bennett's Statement respecting a Board for England . 26
    Letter to be addressed to each Licensing Body . . . 27-9
COOMBE LYING-IN HOSPITAL . . . . . (I. Br.) 7-11
COUNCIL, GENERAL MEDICAL, to meet early in 1872, to receive
    Proposals for Conjoint Examinations 50

			PAGE
CRAVEN, Mr., his Studies to be ante-dated . . . (S. Br.)			5
CRISP, Dr., Letter from			15
DAVIDSON, D. C., his Studies to be ante-dated . . . (S. Br.)			5–7
DEATH REGISTRY, Sir D. Corrigan's motion respecting Amendment of the Laws			20
DE REYNA, Dr. RICARDO, to be registered as D.M. and Surg., Univ. Seville, 1850 . . . . . . (E. Br.)			4
EDUCATION, PROFESSIONAL,—			
Report of Committee on			7–13
,, ,, taken as read			22
,, ,, considered . .		. 22–4,	26–7
,, ,, re-committed . . .			29
,, ,, amended . . .			40–49
,, ,, adopted			49
EVANS, T. D. F., his Studies to be ante-dated . (S. Br.)			5
EXAMINATIONS, PRELIMINARY,—			
List of recognized Examining Bodies			7
List revised . . . . . . (Ex. C.)			6
EXECUTIVE COMMITTEE,—			
Balloted for			32
To Report on Mode of Procedure in reference to Penal Measures Duties delegated to			53
Business for General Council arranged . . . (Ex. C.)			7
FINANCE COMMITTEE, appointed			3
Report of			32–4
,, Adopted			35
FINES (see "Penalties") remitted			4
FREEMAN'S JOURNAL, Letter to Editor of . . . . (I. Br.)			3–4
,, Letter in, from William Ledger Erson . . (I. Br.)			5–8
GAVIN, Mr., his Petition referred to R. Coll. Phys., Edin. . (S. Br.)			5
GENERAL MEDICAL COUNCIL to meet early in 1872, to receive Proposals for Conjoint Examinations . . .			50
GIBB, DAVID, Case of . . . . (S. Br.)			2
GOODCHILD, FRANCIS, his Studies to be ante-dated . . (E. Br.)			5
GRATUITY to Officer of R. Coll. Phys., Edin. . . (S. Br.)			7–8
GULL, Dr., Member of General Council			2
HODGSON, H. A., his Studies to be ante-dated . . . (E. Br.)			5
HOGG, Mr., his application to be registered as Late Assistant Surgeon in H. E. I. Company's Service, granted . . (E. Br.)			2–4
HOGGAN, GEORGE, his Studies to be ante-dated . . . (S. Br.)			7

INDEX. iii

		PAGE
KELLY, Mr., not to keep up the Type of the Medical Register (Ex. C.)		5
,, Letter from		6
KEMPSTER, WILLIAM HENRY, his appearance before the Council, and acquittal		18-19
Mr. Ouvry submits Evidence to Branch Council	(E. Br.)	2
LECHLOW, H. M., his Studies to be ante-dated . . .	(S. Br.)	7
LITTLE, JAMES, his Studies to be ante-dated . . .	(S. Br.)	5
LOWE, EDWIN, his name removed from the Register		13-14
MAC ANDREW, C. M., his Studies to be ante-dated . .	(S. Br.)	7
MASON, Dr., no Public Action to be taken against him .	(E. Br.)	2
MEHAMS, A. E., his Application for Examination rejected .	(S. Br.)	5
MELBOURNE, Letter from the Vice-Chancellor of the University respecting Preliminary Examinations . .	(Ex. C.)	6
MINUTES, Eighth Vol., for 1870, to be Printed . . .	(Ex. C.)	3
MORRIS, FREDERICK HENRY, Certificate of his having been convicted of a Misdemeanour		14
,, his name to be erased from the Register		31
OUVRY, Mr., attends E. Branch Council respecting two cases of Complaint against Registered Practitioners .	(E. Br.)	2
PATTISON, Dr. JOHN, his Petition to be reinstated on the Register not acceded to		14
PEARCE, F. C., his Studies to be ante-dated. . . .	(E. Br.)	5
PENAL MEASURES, Mode of Procedure in		32
PENALTIES imposed on John Underhill remitted . . .	(E. Br.)	4
PENALTY recovered from Chadwick remitted . . .	(S. Br.)	6-7
PHARMACOPŒIA COMMITTEE,—		
Report of		37
,, adopted		38
Committee re-appointed		38
POOR LAW COMMISSIONERS (IRELAND), Letter to .	(I. Br.)	9-11
PORTER at 32, Soho Square, Gratuity to		53
PRESIDENT, Thanks to, for his efficient Services . . .		54
QUAIN, RICHARD, Esq., Member of General Council . . .		2
QUAIN, Dr., elected Member of Executive Committee.	(Ex. C.)	2
RETURNS from Bodies in Schedule (A) of Professional Examinations, and Registration of Students		3
Committee on, appointed		3
Report of Committee		50-2
Referred to Executive Committee		52

INDEX.

	PAGE
REGISTER, THE MEDICAL, for 1871, to be published . . (Ex. C.)	2
Report of Measures respecting Reduction of the Expense of Publishing . . . . (Ex. C.)	2-3
To be Printed by the Stationery Office, of which Notice to be given to Mr. Kelly . . . . . . (Ex. C.)	3, 5
RETURNS from the Medical Departments of the Army and India Office	3-7
Committee on	16
Report of Committee	35-6
,, ,, adopted	37
RUMSEY, Dr., Resigns his Appointment to the General Council (E. Br.)	2

SHARPEY, Dr., Thanks to, for services as Treasurer	35
,, re-appointed as Member of the Medical Council . (S. Br.)	4
STANDING ORDERS AND REGULATIONS (see end) . . . pp.	1-16
Contents of	p. 2
STUDENTS, List of, for 1870, to be Printed . . . . (Ex. C.)	3
Application from a Student to be excused from Examination in Latin, not acceded to . . . . . . (E. Br.)	2
SYDNEY INFIRMARY, NEW SOUTH WALES, Letters from Secretaries of	15-16

| TRAIL, J. W. H., his Studies to be ante-dated . . (S. Br.) | 1 |

VISITATIONS OF EXAMINATIONS,—	
To be re-commenced	38
Committee on	38
,, re-appointed	38
Report of Committee	52-3
Consideration of Report referred to next Meeting of the Council	53

WILLIAMS, WILLIAM H., his Studies to be ante-dated . (E. Br.)	5
WOOD, Dr. ANDREW, Thanks to, for Services as Chairman of Business Committee	54
WOODBURN, W. H., his application as to Student Registration rejected . . . . (S. Br.)	5

www.ingramcontent.com/pod-product-compliance
Lightning Source LLC
Chambersburg PA
CBHW020125170426
43199CB00009B/639